ISBN: 01911977066

Wings of Color fill the Sky,

A happy Song, a joyful Cry,

Spirits lift, old Dreams Renew,

When Birds take Wing,

Our Hearts soar Too.

Anonymous

Blackbird

RED-WINGED BLACKBIRD

YEAR-ROUND * ⬦ **

The Red-winged Blackbird is one of the most common birds in the U.S. and is found in every state. Its most striking feature is the colorful patch on the wing of the male. This patch is called an "epaulet" by ornithologists (from the French word "epaulette," meaning a shoulder ornament on a military uniform). Sometimes the patch is concealed by black feathers so that only a yellow fringe is visible.

During the breeding season in spring and summer, the Red-winged Blackbird will take up a position atop a tall bush or cattail and spend most of the day defending its territory against other birds. But during fall and winter, Red-winged Blackbirds form "mixed foraging flocks" with other blackbirds. During this period they are not territorial, but range over wide areas in their daily search for food. It is common to see such a flock swoop down into a yard or picnic area, gobble up all the food in sight, and then take off for greener pastures elsewhere.

Juvenile Red-winged Blackbirds resemble the adult females. This is usually the case when the male and female adult birds of a species are very different in appearance.

If there is a surplus of females, Red-winged Blackbirds are sometimes polygynous. One male may establish nests with several different females.

* Indicates the time of year when this bird is most frequently seen in Florida.
** Indicates that this bird will come to a seed feeder.

2

Female

△ The female is strikingly different from the male in shape and color and is easily mistaken for a large sparrow.

The Red-winged Blackbird makes a loud and distinctive "chuck" or "check" sound when disturbed.

Other blackbirds in Florida include the Brown-headed Cowbirds and the grackles, but not the crows, which belong to a different bird family even though they are also black.

△ The spreading of the tail feathers by this female is called a "song-spread display." It is a threat used to defend territory (primarily against other females of her own species).

The Attack!

The photographer who snapped these three shots had stopped on a small wooden bridge to photograph a waterbird (visible at left in the first photo).

Angered by this intrusion, the Red-winged Blackbird landed on the automobile mirror to investigate. He then launched an attack, pecking the photographer's arm and driving him further inside the car. While standing defiantly on the window, he spotted his own image in the car mirror and leapt to attack again. After several tries and no success at vanquishing the image, he took off. The photographer also fled to avoid further assaults.

It is quite unusual for a Red-winged Blackbird to attack a human. It is more typical of mockingbirds, which frequently dive at humans and pets.

Like a Window Shade

When the Red-winged Blackbird gets excited, small muscles raise a few black feathers revealing the bright red feathers underneath. The red patches show the bird's alarm upon discovering an intruder on its territory. They are also displayed as a part of the courtship ritual in spring. Researchers who captured some Red-winged Blackbirds and covered their red patches found that the poor birds lost their territories and were unable to attract mates.

△ This photo shows the patch partially covered. The breeding season is over and the red feathers have molted leaving only a dull orange color.

Because of its fascinating red patch, this bird is sometimes simply called a "red-wing," even though the entire wing is not red.

Bluebird

EASTERN BLUEBIRD

This lovely creature is called the "bluebird of happiness" because of its wonderful color, beautiful song and because its arrival in the northern states announces the beginning of spring. It is a quiet, gentle bird, never raucous like some of the other backyard favorites.

The blue color is truly intense. The American philosopher Henry David Thoreau, a great admirer of the bluebird, wrote that this bird "carries the sky on its back." The Pilgrims are said to have called it the "blue robin" in homage to one of the best-loved European birds. There is an Indian legend that this bird was once a dull color, but because of its gentleness, the gods allowed it to bathe in a sacred lake of incredibly blue water and the bluebird emerged from the bath with its striking plumage.

The bluebird, like the robin, is a member of the thrush family. Although its brilliant color bears no resemblance to the more familiar thrushes, the nestling bluebirds are heavily speckled on the breast just like the young of many other thrushes.

Bluebirds nest in holes in trees or fence posts. They are under pressure from starlings and house sparrows for nesting space. Bird lovers are providing specially designed nesting boxes to insure that their population does not decline.

Male

Female

The bluebird is not a backyard bird. Since it eats mostly insects, it is not attracted to feeders. It can be seen sitting on fence posts around open fields, especially fields at the edge of pine woods and around pastures.

How Can Birds Perch Safely on Power Lines?

Electric current will not flow from a power wire unless the wire makes a connection with a "ground". Insulators prevent power wires from touching metal support poles, so the flow of electricity continues along the wire without traveling to the ground. Since a bird's body is not as good a conductor as a wire, electricity will not flow through its body when it perches on a power line, but will take the easier route through the wire without harming the bird. However, if a bird touches a wire and a pole at the same time, it will complete the connection with the ground and the bird may be electrocuted.

Bobwhite

COMMON BOBWHITE   `YEAR-ROUND`

The Bobwhite is Florida's only quail. It is a game bird and can be legally hunted when in season.

A ground dweller, it is commonly seen in pine forests among the palmettos and scrub plants. Hikers will frequently flush whole families which run from one hiding place to another. If really threatened, one of the parents may try to distract the intruder by running into an open clearing while its family disperses in the underbrush.

When families of Bobwhite roost for the night, they cluster together in a circle facing outward with their bodies touching. This "wagon-train" formation helps conserve warmth and allows a watch for predators in all directions.

At the end of the breeding season, several Bobwhite families may band together to form a small flock. These groups are called "coveys." Their members benefit from the protection of greater numbers.

The most obvious features of the Bobwhite are the small head and plump body. The adult male has a white throat and a white stripe above the eye. In the female, these areas are brownish.

This bird says its name. The call is a very clear and distinctive "Bob-WHITE!"

The Bobwhite comes into yards and can be tamed. A good way to encourage the Bobwhite is to spill some seed on the ground at the bottom of your feeder.

Florida Game Birds

Birds which can be legally hunted in Florida are divided into two classes: upland birds, and waterfowl. The upland game birds include the Bobwhite, Turkey, Common Moorhen, Common Coot, Rail, Mourning Dove, White-winged Dove, Snipe and Woodcock. The seasons change each year depending upon bird population estimates. A Florida license is required and the hunter must have the landowner's permission, must be outside any bird sanctuary, and 500 feet or more from any residence. For migratory waterfowl, a federal license is required.

Female

Male

Buntings

Male Painted Bunting

PAINTED BUNTING
INDIGO BUNTING

Buntings are relatives of cardinals and sparrows and are relatively shy birds. They will come to a feeder but feel more comfortable if there is plenty of under-brush available so they can quickly hide if threatened.

The name "bunting" may come from the German word "bunt," meaning "speckled," as some species of buntings are speckled.

The adult male Painted Bunting is one of the most spectacular birds in the world with its brilliant combination of a blue head and bright red breast. The male Indigo Bunting is also quite special with its remarkably deep blue color.

Most of Florida's buntings are re-stricted to small areas of the state. They are found in the southern part of Florida during the winter. They also show up at feeders along the Atlantic coast. During the summer they are found only in the extreme northeast part of Florida.

Male Painted Bunting

The male Indigo Bunting sings his territorial songs from open places such as utility lines and isolated trees.

Male Indigo Bunting

Cardinal

Male 'Big Red'

Male

NORTHERN CARDINAL YEAR-ROUND

The cardinal may have been named for the way the brilliant plumage of the male resembles the scarlet robes worn by Catholic cardinals. The crest of feathers on the head and the jet-black mask on the face help make the cardinal one of the most spectacular of all the backyard birds.

Cardinals love sunflower seeds and will pick them out if a variety of seeds is offered at a feeder. Their heavy, powerful beaks are very effective for cracking hard shells. Although the adults eat mostly seeds, baby cardinals are fed insects by their parents.

Cardinals are very romantic birds, at least during the breeding season in the spring. They are usually seen in pairs and have an extensive variety of courtship rituals. The male will offer bits of food to the female at a feeding station. At other times of the year the male may be indifferent or even drive the female away from the feeder. But, during the spring, the pair will become very close.

The male may stretch his neck, raise his crest, and sway side to side as he sings to the female, and the female will answer with her own song. Both male and female cardinals sing. This is true of some other species also, but in most bird species, only the male birds sing.

Female

Female

The female cardinal does all the nest-building work. The male will bring her food and feed it to her so she doesn't have to stop working until the nest is completed. Cardinals can raise up to four broods per year under good conditions.

Cardinals are very territorial and will chase other birds away from a feeder. They are also known for their attacks against windows which reflect their own images. The attacking cardinal imagines that the reflected image is another cardinal invading his territory. There are several ways of discouraging such attacks. Try soaping the window so that it is not so reflective. Other possibilities include hanging an owl image in the window or putting a rubber snake on the sill. If nothing is done, the attacks might continue throughout the nesting season.

Both males and females have the large, distinctive, pointed crest on the tops of their heads. The crest is raised when the bird is alarmed.

The All-Time Champion "State Bird"

The cardinal is the official state bird of seven states: Illinois, Indiana, Kentucky, North Carolina, Ohio, Virginia, and West Virginia. No other bird can claim as much official recognition, but the Western Meadowlark comes close with six states.

A Short-cut for Suet

Almost all the feeder birds will eat suet (hard animal fat from the area of the loins and kidneys). Beef kidney fat is best. Although it will turn black on the edges, it will not spoil and become rancid as easily as other fats.

Here is an easy way to provide fat for birds. Combine 1 cup of bacon drippings, 1 cup of corn meal, 1/2 cup of flour, 1 cup of water, and 1 tablespoon of sugar. Mix together and cook for five minutes. Shape into "muffins" on a cookie sheet and freeze. Store in plastic bags in the freezer.

Land birds do not have adequate mechanisms to remove salt from their bodies, so salty fats like bacon grease are not good for them unless they are mixed with something else. The same goes for peanuts. Raw peanuts are okay, but salted peanuts may be harmful.

Rare albino cardinal

Catbird

GRAY CATBIRD WINTER

This all-gray bird is best known for its "mewing" cat-like call, most frequently heard when the bird is disturbed or irritated. It has a range of more musical songs, which it sings when it is in a good mood. It is also a skilled mimic of other birds. This is not surprising since the catbird is a close relative of the mockingbird.

The catbird usually stays hidden in heavy brush, but loves to bathe and can be attracted to a garden with a bird bath.

◁ This photo shows the dark marking on the top of the catbird's head. If you are looking for exciting color, try another species.

The catbird will not eat seed at a feeder but can be attracted with fruit. Half an orange is quite a treat.

No Florida birds regularly eat whole oranges on trees. If they did, the Citrus Commission would probably chase them out of the state. There have been reports of Red-bellied Woodpeckers pecking into fruit to get at the seeds.

Baby Carolina Chickadees

CAROLINA CHICKADEE YEAR-ROUND

This bird is a southern version of the Black-capped Chickadee. It looks quite similar to the northern bird but does not have white edges on its wing feathers. The Carolina Chickadee is usually seen only as far south as central Florida. The chickadee says its name when it calls "chick-a-dee-dee-dee." Male and female chickadees are almost identical. Both male and female birds sing. This is unusual for a species in which male and female birds so closely resemble each other.

Chickadees are not afraid of people and are easily attracted to feeders, especially by sunflower seeds. They are very acrobatic and have no trouble using the hanging type of feeder.

Cowbird

BROWN-HEADED COWBIRD

 YEAR-ROUND

These birds get their name from their close association with cows. Cowbirds follow cattle around pastures in the same manner as Cattle Egrets. The movement of the big animals stirs up insects in the grass which the cowbirds catch. They are especially fond of grasshoppers.

These recent invaders of Florida have just started breeding here in small numbers. However, they are common residents during winter.

The female cowbird looks very different from the male, almost like a different species. This strong male-female difference is a common characteristic of many blackbird species, including the Red-winged Blackbirds and the grackles.

Male

Female

Baby Cowbird screaming for attention

Ungrateful Stepchildren

The baby cowbirds do not follow the habits of their foster parents but join other cowbirds as soon as they are old enough to leave the nest.

Cowbird chick being fed by foster parent, a Blue-winged Warbler.

The Foster Parent Plan

The cowbird is a "nest parasite." It lays its eggs in the nests of other birds. Cardinals are common victims in Florida, as are Red-winged Blackbirds and many other species. The cowbird is the only land bird in the United States with this trait. There are a few ducks that parasitize nests, and it is a common behavior among cuckoos in many other parts of the world. The cuckoos in Florida only rarely use the nests of other birds.

Most of the birds chosen as foster parents will tolerate the extra egg and treat the hatchling as one of their own. However, cowbird eggs hatch quickly and the baby cowbird frequently out-grows and out-eats the offspring of the host birds. The cowbird chick is often the only survivor.

Not all birds will accept a cowbird egg laid in their nest. The response varies with the species. The birds of some species will remove the egg, some will abandon or rebuild the nest, and some will even build another nest layer right on top of the cowbird egg.

Crane

SANDHILL CRANE [YEAR-ROUND]

Cranes are among the tallest birds in the world. They are capable of flying at great heights. Some species regularly migrate over the Himalayas. In Chinese and Japanese art and culture, the crane is a much-loved symbol of fidelity, longevity, and grace.

Florida's Sandhill Crane is an impressive sight seldom missed when traveling through the open grasslands of Central Florida. Because of its tall stature and the red crown on its head, the Sandhill Crane can often be spotted from a car at a great distance.

Juvenile

Parents with babies

Sandhill Cranes mate for life and are very attentive parents, helping their chicks forage for food until they are quite well developed.

▷ Most crane couples reinforce their pair bonds with synchronized, ballet-like ritual dances consisting of dipping and bowing, leaping, stretching, and synchronized calls.

Cranes-vs-Herons

Herons, especially Florida's Great Blue Heron, are often mistakenly called "cranes." One difference is that true cranes, such as the Sandhill Crane, fly with their necks fully outstretched. Herons fold their necks during flight (except on take-off).

Crows

AMERICAN CROW, FISH CROW

Not Blackbirds

YEAR-ROUND

Although black in color, crows are not blackbirds. They belong to a different family from the true blackbirds. In Florida, the true blackbirds are Red-winged Blackbirds, grackles, and cowbirds. Crows belong to the same family as jays and ravens. There are no ravens in Florida, but the very common Blue Jays are close relatives.

Two Kinds (but you might not notice)

There are two species of crows in Florida, the American Crow (also called the Common Crow) and the Fish Crow. Even experts cannot always tell the two apart visually. Outside of Florida the Fish Crow is usually found in coastal areas and around fresh water while the Common Crow prefers drier places. The division of crow territories is different in Florida. Here the Common Crows are more likely to be found in rural and wilderness areas and the Fish Crows appear in the populated parts of the state. The Common Crow is the "official" crow of the Everglades National Park. They dominate this territory and visitors to the park will see many of them.

Different Voices

The two crows can be identified by their voices. The "caw" sound of the Fish Crow is slightly different from that of the Common Crow. It is rather nasal and sounds more like "Cah." Fish Crows and American Crows do not usually mix, so a group of crows will most likely all be of the same species. Experts identify them mostly by the sound of their calls.

Really Smart

The crow family may contain the most highly evolved birds in terms of intelligence. The cleverness of crows is legendary. This intelligence is put to use in foraging for food. The curious crow will investigate any possible new source of food such as a discarded sandwich inside a plastic wrapper. A crow would be more likely to figure out how to remove the wrapper than any other bird. Crows will store food in inconspicuous places whenever there is surplus available and will try to keep the caches hidden by covering them with any available materials.

A Lovable Bird?

In spite of their bold, blustering ways, crows have many endearing characteristics, at least in human terms. Most crows mate for life. They look after their offspring longer than most other birds, training them until they have learned all the wily ways necessary to succeed as a crow. They are extremely loyal and the whole flock will come to the aid of a wounded crow. Recordings of crow distress calls have been used by hunters to lure and slaughter large numbers of crows. The crow can make a wide range of sounds in addition to the well known "caw," and pet crows can be trained to talk quite well.

▷ The call of the crow welcomes a new day from the top of a tall cypress tree in the Everglades.

△ Crows have feathers extending down over their beaks and covering their nostrils.

Cuckoos

The Smooth-billed Ani is most frequently seen in South Florida, but is not common in the Everglades. It likes brushy overgrowth as well as fields and groves. Small flocks of anis forage together for insects, especially grasshoppers.

"Ani" is pronounced "Ah-Nee." It is the Spanish pronunciation of a South American Indian word.

This large black bird with the enormous, black, parrot-like beak may not look like the other Florida cuckoos, but it is a member of the same family and does share with them the same unusual toe arrangement (two toes in front and two in back). The famous roadrunner of the American west, another member of the cuckoo family, also has this toe arrangement.

In contrast, most perching birds have three toes in front and one behind. This is a practical arrangement which allows both perching and hopping.

The Ani is of special interest to visiting birders because Florida is the only state in the country where it can be found. There is, however, a very similar species called the Groove-billed Ani which breeds in Texas.

YELLOW-BILLED CUCKOO
MANGROVE CUCKOO

The European cuckoos make the sound for which they are named, but the Florida cuckoos only make the "cuck" without the "coo." The use of the word "cuckoo" to indicate craziness probably relates to the silly behavior of the little birds in cuckoo clocks.

Yellow-billed Cuckoos are found throughout Florida and all over the eastern United States. The Mangrove Cuckoo is a species which has colonized Florida from the West Indies. It is primarily found in South Florida. It is most commonly seen in summer although some birds now stay year-round.

The Yellow-billed Cuckoo has a noticeable yellow coloring in the lower part of its beak. Its breast is pure white. The Mangrove Cuckoo has a black mask over the eyes and a buff-colored breast. Neither bird is commonly seen, so they provide a thrill for birders who are able to spot them.

Cuckoos are known to sing more often on very humid days. High humidity often precedes rain, and some people believe these songs can predict rain. For this reason, Florida's cuckoos have been called "rain crows."

Mangrove Cuckoo

An interesting and attractive feature of the Yellow-billed Cuckoo is that it has feathers extending down its legs.

Some African eagles have this characteristic. They are called "booted" eagles. The Buff Cochin Chicken also has this feathering, as do some species of pigeons.

Doves

Mourning Dove at nest

THE WORLD OF DOVES

Symbols of Peace and Glad Tidings

Doves are known as symbols of peace. In the Bible, Noah received the olive branch from the beak of a dove. Solomon spoke of the joyful time "when the voice of the turtle is heard in the land," referring to the cry of the turtledove. In Christianity, the Lord is sometimes referred to as the "heavenly dove." "Lo, the heavens were opened unto him and he saw the Spirit of God descending like a dove...." Matthew 3:16.

In the Islamic religion, the courtyards surrounding mosques often host large flocks of doves. They are treated with great respect because it is written that Allah communicated some of his wisdom to Mohammed using a dove as the messenger.

A Cranky Bird?

The use of the dove as a symbol of peace and love is somewhat misleading. Although doves look like gentle birds, people with feeders know that the Mourning Dove is very feisty and is always squabbling with other birds.

Doves vs Pigeons

Doves and pigeons belong to the same family and the names are often used interchangeably. Both male and female birds can feed their young "pigeon's milk," which is not really milk. It is a sloughed-off layer of skin tissue from the bird's crop plus whatever food is in the crop (usually a mixture of finely ground and partially digested seeds).

Mourning Doves

MOURNING DOVE

The Mourning Dove is one of the most common and popular backyard birds. The soft "cooing" sound of this bird is most frequently heard early in the morning, often before sunrise. Because of this early morning activity, it is often mistakenly called the "morning dove."

Many people mistake the "cooing" for the voice of an owl. The Mourning Dove was apparently given its name by someone who considered its call "mournful," but many people find the sound soothing and delightful.

Notice that the Mourning Dove bobs its head as it walks and makes an amazingly loud whistling noise with its wings while in flight.

Mourning Doves breed throughout the continental United States and are the target of many hunters. They are lawful game birds in Florida when in season. Dove hunting is considered an important tradition among many old-time Florida families.

When it comes to building a nest, the Mourning Dove is notoriously lazy and will make do with almost any little pile of

sticks. Sometimes Mourning Doves will dispense with nest construction altogether and simply use the remains of another bird's nest, adding a few bits and pieces of their own. Mourning Doves have been known to lay eggs right on the ground with no nest at all.

▷ During the breeding season in the spring, the male Mourning Dove has a patch of iridescent color on each side of the neck. Throughout this period, the coloring of the beautiful blue eye-ring and bright orange legs becomes much more intense.

Baby Mourning Dove "puffing" feathers for extra insulation against the cold.

Doves

ROCK DOVE

 YEAR-ROUND

This is the domestic pigeon commonly seen in parks. A native of Europe and Asia (where it is still a wild species) it was introduced to this continent hundreds of years ago. Varieties of this bird are very popular for racing, especially in Europe.

In the United States, the Rock Dove is usually seen in the cities where it has found ways to co-exist with man and has made a nuisance of itself in many places. The Rock Doves in cities have become very tame and will eat from your hand. However, Rock Doves found outside of cities are just as wild as the other birds.

Doves can suck up water while bending their heads downward. Most birds don't have this ability and must use their beaks to scoop up water and then tilt their heads back in order to swallow.

△ This Rock Dove is sunbathing on a roof. Birds frequently spread their wings to "catch some rays," but not in quest of the perfect tan. More likely, it gives some relief from feather mites. Spreading the wings may cause the mites to move to the shade under the wings where they are more easily removed by preening.

WHITE-CROWNED PIGEON [YEAR-ROUND]

These beautiful birds are seldom seen through most of Florida but are common along the Keys in the summer. They build their nests on uninhabited mangrove islands but do come to populated areas where they feed on wild fruit. They have been over-hunted in the Caribbean but are not legal game in Florida.

GROUND-DOVE [YEAR-ROUND]

This is the smallest dove in the United States. As its name implies, it is usually seen on the ground. The orange color of the beak and the speckled breast help in identification. A dull flash of reddish-orange is visible on the wings during flight.

RINGED TURTLE DOVE [YEAR-ROUND]

This is a domestic bird which has formed a small colony in St. Petersburg north of Mirror Lake and is sometimes seen in the public parks of that city. Several other colonies of birds in South Florida, thought to be Ringed Turtle Doves, were recently discovered to be the very similar Collared Dove.

The Collared Dove is shown in the photo at far right. Note that the tips of its flight feathers are much darker.

Ground Dove

Collared Dove

Ringed Turtle Dove

Finch

AMERICAN GOLDFINCH [WINTER]

Goldfinches breed in the northern states during the summer. They use thistledown in building their nests. Since the northern thistles develop late in the season, the goldfinch is one of the last of the winter residents to arrive in Florida and one of the last to leave.

In Florida, goldfinches do not visit feeders very often because of the abundant natural food. They feast on the tiny seeds from the cones of Australian Pines.

American Goldfinch in winter plumage.

"How to Recognize Your Old Friends from Up North"

The American Goldfinch is famous for the brilliant color of the male, but after breeding in the northern states, goldfinches and many other migrant birds molt and lose their brilliant feathers. On their way south through Florida in the fall, these birds are rather drab and identification becomes difficult. Birders call them "LBJs" or Little Brown Jobs. Fortunately, many of these same birds have their brilliant plumage when they pass through again in the spring on their way to the northern breeding areas.

Flycatchers

Flycatchers spend much of the day perched on branches waiting for insect prey. When an insect appears, they sally forth to catch it in flight. Since they spend much of their time in the tops of trees, birders usually locate them by their calls. As insect eaters, they are not drawn to backyard feeders but can be attracted with drinking water.

SCISSOR-TAILED FLYCATCHER   WINTER

▷ The Scissor-tailed Flycatcher has such distinctive, long, divided tail-feathers that identification is never difficult. It is usually seen with its extraordinary tail-feathers folded together.

Scissor-tailed
Flycatcher

GREAT CRESTED FLYCATCHER   YEAR-ROUND

△ This olive-brown bird with a gray throat is easily identified by its yellow belly and brownish tail. Its loud "WHEEP" call frequently helps birders spot it.

Flycatchers

Eastern
Kingbird

△ Angry Eastern Kingbird, showing the color patch on its head. This patch is usually concealed by other feathers.

△ Gray Kingbirds are only found in Florida and the Carribean. The best place to see them is in the mangroves.

Eastern Phoebe

Acadian Flycatcher with chicks

EASTERN KINGBIRD [SUMMER]
GRAY KINGBIRD [SUMMER]

The kingbirds are so named because of their vigorous defense of their nesting territories.

The Eastern Kingbird and the Gray Kingbird are somewhat similar in appearance. They both have a patch of color on the top of the head which is seldom seen (except when they are alarmed). The Eastern Kingbird has a white band across the tip of its square tail and a white breast. It loves to eat bees and sometimes makes its home near a hive. The Gray Kingbird is paler and has a notched tail. In Florida, it is found most often in coastal areas.

EASTERN PHOEBE [WINTER]

The Eastern Phoebe is a small, active flycatcher which says its name (fee-bee), but is not heard calling very often in Florida. It makes a downward jerking motion with its tail when perched.

ACADIAN FLYCATCHER [SUMMER]

The Acadian Flycatcher has two white wing bars which are handy field markings. It is one of the smallest birds in Florida.

24

Gnatcatcher

BLUE-GRAY GNATCATCHER

YEAR-ROUND

As you might expect, this small bird does catch gnats for a living. It is often seen in the company of titmice and chickadees. It holds its tail raised at a 45 degree angle most of the time.

Its call is high pitched and insect-like. The white ring around the eye is important for identification.

Notice the worm-eaten leaves in this photo. The presence of insects may have attracted the Blue-gray Gnatcatcher to this particular tree.

The Blue-gray Gnatcatcher builds an elegant nest which rests saddle-style on a branch or in a fork. The nest is held together with spider silk and is covered with lichens on the outside for camouflage. It very much resembles the nest of the Ruby-throated Hummingbird

RUBY-CROWNED KINGLET

WINTER

△ Next to the hummingbird, this is the smallest bird found in Florida. It is constantly on the move. Whenever it calls, it jerks its wings almost faster than can be seen. The ruby crown is seldom noticed, except in the spring when the male may display it to attract a female or to threaten another male. Like the Blue-gray Gnatcatcher, it has a white eye-ring.

Care of Orphan Birds

When a baby bird has fallen from the nest, it is best to place the bird back in the nest if possible. It is not true that parents will reject a baby that has been handled by humans. If the nest has been destroyed or cannot be found, create a new nest with a hanging basket and some grass.

If a baby bird is well feathered and can hop around and fly a little, place him in some bushes away from predators. He may be too old to stay in the nest. Bird parents force their young out of the nest as soon as possible because nests are easily located by predators such as garter snakes. The longer a baby bird stays in the nest after he is capable of leaving, the less his chances for survival.

If the parents do not return within a couple of hours, you may decide the baby needs further care. Unfeathered babies can be placed in a box with a heating pad on a low setting (do not cook the bird!). Feathered babies do not need heat and can be placed on newspapers. An emergency formula can be made by mashing hard-boiled egg yolks into a little warm water and administered with an eye dropper when the baby calls for food.

Some birds, especially baby mockingbirds, must have vitamins or they quickly become so weak they cannot perch. Bird vitamins are available at pet stores.

If possible, contact your local wildlife rehabilitation center. Keeping wild birds is against the law. A person whose true purpose is to keep a colorful songster as a pet cage bird can always use the excuse that he was only helping a sick or orphaned bird. Wildlife officers might be strict about enforcing the law if they suspect such a situation.

Grackles

Male Boat-tailed Grackle

BOAT-TAILED GRACKLE YEAR-ROUND

In most states Boat-tailed Grackles are found around water, frequently in the same habitats as Red-winged Blackbirds. But in Florida they are also common in dry areas including populated places. In fact, Florida is the only state where they can be found away from coastal areas. They especially like cattails and tall weeds around lakes, drainage ditches, standing water, wet meadows, and sometimes open fields. They spend their days foraging for insects and seeds.

They don't walk so much as strut, always displaying a proud, haughty bearing.

The male-female differences in the Boat-tailed Grackle are very striking. The female is brown in color and doesn't even look like the same species.

Boat-tailed Grackles are polygynous birds. The males band together in flocks to forage for food, often in the company of Red-winged Blackbirds and Brown-headed Cowbirds. The females visit these flocks and the males may mate with several females. No pair bond is established. The males do not participate in nest building or rearing of the young but may sometimes help defend the nests established by the females.

Female Boat-tailed Grackle

Juvenile

Two Boat-tailed Grackles vocalizing and confronting each other with "bill-tilting" threat displays

Common Grackle

△ This Common Grackle has built a nest using Spanish moss.

COMMON GRACKLE YEAR-ROUND

The Boat-tailed Grackle is more common than the Common Grackle in areas where plenty of fresh water is available. The Boat-tailed Grackle is a much larger bird with a proportionately larger and wider tail (which is partially folded and thought to resemble the keel of a boat). Both birds show a blue iridescent sheen when the light strikes them from the right angle. Otherwise, they may appear to be solid black. Both birds are sometimes mistaken for crows, but grackles are smaller and more slender than crows.

Notice the striking yellow eyes of the Common Grackles which make them stand out from all the other black-colored birds. Boat-tailed Grackles from northern states also have yellow eyes but Florida's resident Boat-tailed Grackles do not. Crows, Red-winged Blackbirds, Brown-headed Cowbirds, and European Starlings all have dark eyes.

Common Grackles do not demand waterfront living like the Boat-tailed Grackles. They are suburban birds and are frequently seen foraging on lawns. They like populated areas and feed on human debris as well as the food nature provides.

When not nesting, grackles tend to roost in remote areas where there are large stands of trees. Colonial groups of thousands will gather together at night.

Hummingbird

Male

RUBY-THROATED HUMMINGBIRD

SUMMER

Hummingbirds are famous for their ability to hover in the air and their great speed and agility. They are the only birds capable of flying backwards with ease. Their name comes from the buzzing sound of their wings which vibrate at up to 70 beats per second. In addition to being the most agile fliers, hummers are also the smallest North American birds.

The male Ruby-throated Hummingbird has a spectacular patch of red color on its throat (when seen from just the right angle). Marks of distinctive color on the throat of a bird are called "gorgets" by ornithologists. This word formerly referred to a piece of armor which protected the throat and later was used to describe necklaces and throat ornaments worn by stylish ladies.

Although there are hundreds of species of hummers in the western hemisphere, the ruby-throated is the only species which breeds in Florida. These birds are attracted to the nectar of certain tubular flowers and help pollinate plants in the same manner as insects. The shrimp plant is one of their favorite nectar sources in Florida gardens. Other plants which may attract hummers are the trumpet creeper vine, honeysuckle, impatiens, and salvia. Hummers are very common in

the Florida Keys during winter where they enjoy nectar from the abundant flowers of the orchid trees.

▷ Hummingbirds use their long tongues to gather nectar and to snare small insects. The hollow tongue design allows hummers to sip nectar as if they were using a straw. Most of their feeding is accomplished while hovering, but with certain flowers, hummers will alight and take a rest. This hummer may be searching for insects rather than nectar in the hibiscus flower.

Female hummer with blue salvia

28

Female

Female

Hummers will also sip sugar water from specially designed feeders. Oddly, hummers in Florida are not very attracted to this kind of feeder. In the southwestern states, sugar-water feeders usually draw many hummingbirds.

During unusually cold weather, hummingbirds may hibernate in a sleep-like state called "torpor" in order to conserve energy. Birds found in this condition are sometimes thought to be dead. In Florida, hummers can be seen after a cold front has passed through perched motionless in torpor early in the morning. Later in the morning when the temperature rises, they will awaken.

The hummingbird nest is a tiny cup attached to the limb of a tree. It is usually less than two inches in diameter. It is constructed of soft fibers held together with spider web material and well camouflaged on the outside with lichens removed from the bark of trees.

Hummer at Nest

A Long-Range Bullet

While some hummers are year-round residents in Florida, most migrate south during the winter to Mexico or Central America. One day, after feeding heavily, the hummer will slowly rise straight up from its perch, pause momentarily, and then streak like a bullet toward the endless horizon of the Gulf of Mexico.

It is amazing that such tiny birds could consume enough fuel for this journey. Yet, they survive over 600 miles of non-stop flight and return in the same manner in the spring. Some arctic terns fly across the Atlantic, but they can stop to feed along the way. There are no tubular flowers available in the Gulf to help the hummers. It is possible that hummers make use of favourable winds and it is known that they sometimes land on ships to rest. But the lengthy flight by the tiny birds still remains a great marvel.

Iridescent Color in Birds

The jewel-like shimmering color that is seen in the feathers of certain birds (such as the throat feathers of the Ruby-throated Hummingbird) is a very special example of nature's beauty. Most ordinary color is produced by pigment. Iridescent color in birds is produced by the structures of certain feathers which act like prisms and break up light into its rainbow hues.

That is why the color is not seen in its full brightness unless viewed at the proper angle. In fact, the Ruby-throated Hummingbird's throat would look almost black if seen from certain angles. If the feathers were plucked from the bird and ground up with a mortar and pestle, the resulting powder would look like mud. The beautiful colors would disappear forever because the prisms would have been destroyed.

Jays

BLUE JAY

YEAR-ROUND

Blue Jays are members of the crow family and, like the crows, are very clever birds. They are best known for their bold, aggressive manner. A jay will chase pets, plunder eggs from the nests of other birds, and generally dominate the entire backyard. Jays do benefit the other smaller birds in at least one way. They will harass owls and hawks and often save small birds at feeders from predation. Mockingbirds do this also.

Like the crows, jays stash excess food in safe places for future use. Nuts and seeds are often hidden. For this reason, Florida Blue Jays are frequently seen dashing around in the abundant oak trees. They gather acorns and store many of them just like squirrels. In addition to the nuts and seeds, jays will eat just about any food that is available.

Although there are plenty of year-round resident Blue Jays, in the winter the population really swells as many Blue Jays from the northern states migrate to Florida.

Jays are known for their curiosity

The Joys of "Anting"

Blue Jays and a number of other birds have been observed flying to ant hills, allowing the ants to climb around on their feathers, and then using their beaks to rub the tiny ants all over their bodies. It is thought that the formic acid from the bodies of the ants works like a natural insecticide to relieve the problem of feather mites.

After the nesting season is finished baby Blue Jays will remain with their family group during the fall until they are full grown.

Blue Jay

SCRUB JAY

YEAR-ROUND

The Scrub Jay differs from the Blue Jay in several ways. It has no crest on its head, its back is brown-colored, and it lacks the white wing-markings.

The Scrub Jay is not a backyard bird like the Blue Jay. It is limited to a number of small areas in Florida with dry sandy soil that supports scrub oak trees. It has some very interesting habits and is one of the species most eagerly sought by birders visiting Florida.

The Scrub Jay has an unusual social system. Most songbirds never interact with their parents after leaving the nest, but the young Scrub Jays remain around their nest after they have matured and help their parents feed the young of later broods. These young birds are called "helpers" by researchers and have been likened to the young "helpers" in the family groups of wolves.

Why should Scrub Jays behave so differently from other birds in this regard? The Scrub Jay is so rigidly restricted to living in the scrub oak environment and this environment is so limited that, ordinarily, all suitable nesting territory is fully in use. So, the young birds must wait until a breeding bird dies, or until they are able to expand their parents' territory through competition with the other breeding birds. Young Scrub Jays probably increase their chances of survival by remaining with their families during this waiting period.

Scrub Jay

Nesting Scrub Jays

Killdeer

Broken Wing Display

KILLDEER

`YEAR-ROUND`

The Killdeer looks a lot like a sand-piper but is a member of the Plover group. They are found throughout the state, not just in the coastal areas. The funny name comes from the bird's plaintive cry.

Killdeers like open fields and meadows, but a couple of vacant lots in a housing subdivision might be sufficient habitat. They are not, however, a back-yard bird (unless, of course, your back-yard is the Kissimmee Prairie).

The Killdeer is best known for its broken wing act. The Killdeer lays its eggs in open depressions on sandy ground or grassy fields. If an animal or human approaches the eggs, the Killdeer will try to lead the intruder away by dropping a wing, making a lot of noise, and hobbling so as to appear injured and easy prey. The scientific species name, *vociferus*, is some indication of this bird's ability to attract attention.

There is a fascinating variation to this "distraction display." If the intruder is an animal such as a cow, the Killdeer will fly up into its face until it turns away from the nest. The Killdeer seems to realise that a cow cannot be distracted by a broken wing act in the same manner as a man or a dog.

The Breeding Bird Atlas Project

When you renew a driver's license, the application form allows you to check off a dollar contribution for Florida's non-game wildlife. This fund is administered by the Florida Game and Fresh Water Fish Commission and part of the money is now financing a five year study of breeding birds coordinated by the Florida Audubon Society. The state has been divided into small sectors and skilled amateurs assigned to study each sector and report the number of nests of each species found and other breeding data.

In addition to documenting which birds are breeding in Florida, the results will be compared with old records and will indicate changes in bird populations and ranges. This information will help document man's effect on the environment and help in future planning.

Martin

Male Martin

Male Martin

PURPLE MARTIN

[SUMMER]

Purple Martins are swallows. They are among the first birds to arrive in Florida in late winter and early spring. The male is solid black with an iridescent blue sheen. The female is easily distinguished by her light-colored belly and brownish color. Many people encourage their presence by erecting multi-story bird houses or putting out hollow gourds for nest boxes. Starlings and House Sparrows often inhabit the communal nest boxes intended for Purple Martins.

Female Martin

WDW

SM

A Very Clever Way to Sell Bird Houses

Many people believe that Purple Martins eat zillions of mosquitos. This is a myth created by certain manufacturers of those fancy, multi-story martin houses. They have promoted their products as a means to attract Purple Martins and thus biologically control mosquitos. Although Purple Martins do eat an occasional mosquito, part of their diet consists of dragonflies. Ironically, the main food of the dragonfly is the mosquito. There are many factors controlling the size of mosquito populations. The presence of a Purple Martin house will probably not have much effect either way.

△ Martins sharing multi-story apartment complex with sparrows

Meadowlark

EASTERN MEADOWLARK (YEAR-ROUND)

The meadowlark breeds on the ground in thick grasses, but is frequently seen sitting on tall grasses, utility poles, or wires where it is easily visible.

The meadowlark nest resembles a tunnel of grass. In addition to his breeding nest, the male also constructs many "dummy" nests. The purpose of the extra nests is not clear. He may use them just for shelter, to distract predators, or possibly to attract a mate.

The bright colors inside the mouths of baby meadowlarks act as a target and a stimulus for the parent birds to feed the babies. These colorful mouths are common among the young of those species which are born helpless (altricial birds). Birds that are born self-sufficient (precocial birds) and can feed themselves lack these bright "target" colors.

▷ A distinctive feature is the black "V" shaped marking across the bright yellow breast.

34

▷ The meadowlark's call is one of the most pleasant melodies of spring.

Fecal Sacs

Amazingly, the waste material (bird droppings) excreted by bird nestlings comes wrapped in thin watertight membranes. These little packages are easily removed from the nest by the parent birds. Some parents actually swallow the fecal sacs since the baby birds do not do a very good job of digestion and there is still quite a bit of food value left in them.

▷ Note the beautiful pattern on the meadowlark's back and white patch on each side of its tail. Despite its brilliant color, the Eastern Meadowlark is a member of the blackbird family. This classification is based upon anatomy rather than outward appearance.

Mockingbird

NORTHERN MOCKINGBIRD

`YEAR-ROUND`

The scientific name, *Mimus polyglottos,* means "mimic of many tongues," a good description of the State Bird of Florida.

The "mocker" is a superb songster with many beautiful melodies of its own as well as the ability to imitate the songs of other birds and any man-made noises that come to its attention.

A World-Class Performer

Many experts consider the mockingbird to be the finest songbird in the world in terms of its huge repertoire and number of performances given. There is a theory that birds that are ordinary in color are more gifted in song. The mockingbird is often cited as an example.

Property Rights

Mockingbirds are very territorial. They establish and defend a breeding territory around their nests in the spring and a food-gathering territory in the fall. Their prolific songs help to mark and establish these territories.

The "Haves" Versus the "Have-Nots"

The "landed-gentry," those mockingbirds with established territories, seem capable of recognizing a common interest. They will sometimes set aside their bickering and band together for a few moments to help a neighboring mocker repel an intruder who has no territory!

Mockers are famous for attacking intruders ·to their nesting territories. Their targets include cats, dogs, squirrels, and people, as well as other birds. Their diving attacks have reduced many a household pet to a nervous wreck when the poor animal merely ventured into its own backyard.

△ Mockers benefit other small bird species by harassing large birds. Here a mocker chases a crow.

△ The eggs of mockingbirds are among the most beautiful in the bird world. The delicate blue color is perfectly complimented by the soft brown spots.

They Sing at Night

A few Florida birds can be heard singing after dark. The mockingbird may sit in the same tree and continue his music all night long. Studies have shown that only unmated males sing at night, although it is not known for sure that the purpose of the song is to attract a mate.

Other Florida night singers are the Bobwhite, Common Nighthawk, Chuck-wills-widow, Whip-poor-will, and the Killdeer.

Wing-Flashing

Mockingbirds sit on a perch and observe a yard or an open field. When opportunity knocks, the mocker will fly down from its perch to the ground and dash about, frequently spreading its wings. There is a large white patch on each wing, and it is thought that by flashing these bright spots, the mockingbird frightens insects, causing them to jump and reveal their locations.

Some researchers have suggested other functions for wing-flashing such as territorial defense. The true nature of this behavior is still debated.

A curious baby Northern Mockingbird

The Case of the Bigamous Mocker

Bigamy is unusual with mockingbirds, but, as with humans, it is not unknown. A university researcher followed the marital stress endured by one sexually ambitious mockingbird during an entire breeding season. This bird had established two nests with different mates, but feeding the young of both was too much burden for one bird to bear. He chose to feed the young of one female for a while and then abruptly switched to the other rather than trying to support both at the same time.

The resulting hardship to the young birds who were only fed by their mother caused some loss of nestlings. However, researchers noted that this male was more aggressive than average. His success in defending both nests against intruders may have made up for his inability to feed both sets of young.

Why did the second female choose a male who was already mated (although unmated males were available)? Her decision may have been influenced by the male's unusual aggressiveness. Her choice of such a mate may have actually increased the chances for survival of her chicks.

The "Border Dance"

Two mockers will meet eye to eye along the boundary line between their territories. They will jump from side to side, each following the other's movements, reaffirming the boundaries, and then, usually, each will fly back into its own territory without a fight.

Oriole

NORTHERN ORIOLE

 MIGRANT

This bird used to be known as the Baltimore Oriole, but ornithologists decided that it should be included in the same species as a very similar western bird formerly called Bullock's Oriole. Now both birds have been grouped together and are simply called Northern Orioles.

Orioles are seen as migrants in Florida, just passing through in the fall on their way to South America and returning in the spring.

Northern Oriole

ORCHARD ORIOLE

 MIGRANT

The Orchard Oriole is smaller than the Northern Oriole. It is also darker and more reddish-brown

◁ In the north where Orioles breed, they are famous for their carefully constructed hanging nests.

Orchard Oriole

Parrots

AND OTHER EXOTICS

PARAKEETS

 YEAR-ROUND

Nest boxes for budgies

The most familiar parakeet is the Budgerigar, or "budgie," which is commonly kept as a house pet. The budgie was originally imported from Australia. It is bred commercially in the United States and in recent years has become the most popular cage bird.

In Florida, flocks of budgies are found in the wild. These birds are descendants of parakeets that escaped captivity or were intentionally released. They are most common along the Gulf Coast, especially in Pinellas County, and are frequently seen perched on telephone wires with starlings. At dusk, hundreds (sometimes thousands) will settle into a single tree to roost for the night. Budgies may be common in an area for a few years and then suddenly disappear completely as the flock moves to a new area.

In the wild, breeding budgies have reverted to their natural color, which is green. The colors seen in pet shops are the result of selective breeding by man.

When the birds are allowed to make their own choices of mates, the dominant genes which produce the green color will cause the following generations to be largely green.

If you see blue, white, or yellow budgies perched with a predominantly green flock, the odd-colored birds are most likely recent "escapes" that have not been bred in the wild. Likewise, a lone bird or pair of birds are probably escapes which have not yet found a flock.

There are a number of other birds of the parrot family which are sometimes seen in Florida. These include the Monk Parakeet, the Canary-winged Parakeet, and the Black-hooded Conure. South Florida has more than 20 species of "parrot-like" escapes flocking throughout the Miami area. The Monk Parakeets have constructed huge communal nests on telephone poles.

Male budgies have blue color around their nostrils, females have buff color.

△ This Red-whiskered Bulbul (not a member of the Parrot family) belongs to a small colony in Miami.

△ This Black-headed Conure is a member of a small colony in North Shore Park, St. Petersburg, and is also found in the Miami area.

The Great Escape

There are many exotic birds (non-native birds) roaming around South Florida. They are mostly the descendants of birds brought into the country by zoos and exotic pet importers. A few of these birds get away from their masters, establish small, self-sustaining colonies, and sometimes become fully naturalized residents.

Birders call them "escapes" (not "escapees" as with prison convicts). Bird "listers" add them to their "life lists" just the same as any other bird once they have become established in the wild.

The consequences of new introductions to the natural community are difficult to predict. Some species, such as the European Starling (which was intentionally introduced), become major threats to local birds by competing for food and nesting space. Others, such as the budgies and Ringed Turtle Doves, find their own niche and prosper without displacing other birds.

Budgies and Ringed Turtle Doves may be harmless because they are so localized and so dependent upon humans. In both cases, residents of the areas where they are found have provided food and bird houses. Their impact on other birds might be different if they were able to expand their range.

There is concern that the budgies might expand their range into the central part of the state and become a threat to certain crops. If this should happen, there will surely be a battle between the agricultural interests that are threatened and the numerous retirees who enjoy having these beautiful birds in their backyards.

In most cases "escapes" do not survive, or do not survive in sufficient numbers to reproduce. Some of the more adaptable "escapes" establish small colonies in the most hospitable areas and do not expand their range. Most of the "escapes" that have established small breeding colonies in Florida belong to the parrot family.

Worse than a trip to the dentist!

It is not true that splitting the tongue or removing the tongue will help birds learn to talk. However, many people believe that it does help, and in parts of Asia, there are professional "de-tongue-ers" who earn their livings by traveling from place to place to remove the tongues of pet birds.

Robin

AMERICAN ROBIN

The robin is mostly a winter visitor to Florida, but has been found breeding as far south as Tampa. It is common to see large numbers of robins during winter. Like most of our visitors, they have a really good time here. They gorge themselves on the bright red berries of the Brazilian pepper and get totally drunk! There are frequent reports of robins staggering across lawns, unable to fly.

Female with worms

Male

Robins can be seen tilting their heads to one side while hunting worms. This may give them improved forward-looking vision for grasping their prey.

Robins are members of the thrush family and, like many thrushes, have young which are heavily spotted.

Even the Word Itself Looks Like a Box of Eggs!

Oology is the collection and study of bird eggs. It was a very popular hobby in the previous century, but impossible now because of the laws protecting wild birds and their nests. However, surviving egg collections and notes taken by the collectors have helped present-day ornithologists in a number of ways. For example, to determine whether a species has declined in numbers, ornithologists may seek records kept by oologists a hundred years ago to get some indication of the number of bird nests in certain areas. Another valuable use of these collections is to determine the thickness of eggshells prior to the use of pesticides such as DDT. Although egg collecting is illegal in England, there are still more than 600 known "eggers" in that country who flout the law and risk prosecution to pursue their hobby. Penalties can include confiscation of their collections, their vehicles, and jail. One egger whose truck had been confiscated was recently interviewed after being released from jail. While the interview was being conducted he was diligently at work constructing a wooden cabinet with dozens of drawers only a few inches deep with each drawer divided into hundreds of small, egg-sized compartments. When asked the purpose of the cabinet he replied that he was going to use it to "store his pants."

Shrike

LOGGERHEAD SHRIKE `YEAR-ROUND`

The shrike is famous for its habit of storing food on sharp hooks and has earned the nickname "butcher bird." The shrike will capture insects and small animals and hang them up on any available sharp object. In northern states, the sharp thorn of a tree or bush is commonly used (hawthorn is a favorite). Shrikes are among the very few North American songbirds that are regular predators of small mammals, birds and lizards.

The shrike has a sharply hooked beak which helps capture live prey, and a close view reveals black whiskers. From a distance, a shrike could be confused with a mockingbird, but shrikes have heavy black masks over their eyes and a more compact shape.

The flight of the shrike is distinctive. When flying from perch to perch, the shrike will drop suddenly to nearly ground level, fly the distance close to the ground, and then ascend sharply to the new perch.

Shrikes are not large birds, but they are powerful enough to capture prey the size of mice in addition to insects. Shrikes often fight with mockingbirds because the two are very much alike and nest in the same areas.

In Florida, the shrike relies heavily on barbed wire fences for its meat-rack. If you notice an insect impaled on the points of a barbed wire fence, there is very likely a Loggerhead Shrike working this territory.

The name "shrike" probably comes from the word "shriek" because of this bird's harsh call.

41

Snipe

COMMON SNIPE   [WINTER]

Many people think there is no such thing as a snipe because of a traditional prank played on children arriving at summer camp for the first time. The newcomers are given a bag and sent out into the darkness with instructions to "catch a snipe." They return exhausted and empty-handed hours later to the jeers of the older campers.

Snipes really do exist but they are hard to find even by experienced birders searching in broad daylight. They usually live around ponds and other wet areas where they probe the ground with their long beaks searching for worms and grubs. When flushed, they will scream "SNIPE" and fly off in a zig-zag pattern.

The Snipe is a gamebird in Florida and may be legally hunted in the proper season.

Sparrows

HOUSE SPARROW   [YEAR-ROUND]

The bird most people think of as a sparrow is not really a sparrow at all, but a member of the Weaver Finch family. This is the House Sparrow, sometimes called the English Sparrow. It was introduced from Europe in the 1850's and, like the starling, has become one of the most common birds in the United States.

House Sparrows are especially common around man. Visitors to Florida might think that they live primarily around motel swimming pools and exist on a diet of leftover potato chips and french fries. This is not far from the truth. These little birds make good use of man-made environments for both food and shelter.

In the wilds of Africa, these birds produce woven nests. But in this country, the House Sparrow confines itself to nesting near man, using man-made structures for nest sites and human trash for food. Sometimes large shaggy nests are found in trees, but they are not well made like those of the House Sparrow's African kin.

Male

Male (left) and female

The All-Electric Home
House Sparrows frequently nest inside lighted outdoor signs. These nests must be nice and warm in winter. Any small opening which allows access to a building or man-made structure will invite a sparrow family to set up house-keeping.

42

Sparrows

Other Sparrows

There is not much grain grown in Florida, so there are not many grain-eating birds, such as sparrows, living here. Seaside Sparrows eat insects and the House Sparrows eat human trash, but the other sparrows can't afford to stay in Florida for long.

CHIPPING SPARROW WINTER

▷ A winter visitor that will come to feeders. They are common at picnic tables and are very tame.

Front view

Back view

SONG SPARROW WINTER

△ The Song Sparrow is an uncommon winter visitor. This bird was the subject of a classic study of behavior published in the 1930's by Margaret Nice.

WHITE-THROATED SPARROW WINTER

△ The White-throated Sparrow has some of the most beautiful songs of any bird. Banding studies have shown that migrating White-throated Sparrows return to the same place every year, sometimes even the same tree or bush.

SAVANNAH SPARROW WINTER

△ This sparrow is common in Florida in the winter. It often hangs around cattle pens in hopes of grabbing some of the grain in the cattle feed.

GRASSHOPPER SPARROW YEAR-ROUND

△ This species is extremly rare as a breeding bird in Florida, but migrant Grasshopper Sparrows from northern states are common in Florida in the winter. Grasshopper Sparrows are hard to see as they stay low and creep through the underbrush. Their song is an insect-like buzz and they sing at night.

MH/Cornell

FIELD SPARROW

The Field Sparrow is common in fields in the panhandle part of the state in winter. It is one of the few sparrows that breeds in Florida (at least in North Florida). The pink bill and white eye-ring makes this bird very attractive and easy to recognize.

SWAMP SPARROW WINTER

▽ This sparrow is common in Florida during the winter. It lives in the swampy areas around rivers and lakes.

KP/VU

SEASIDE SPARROWS YEAR-ROUND

The Seaside Sparrow is a resident of salt marshes along the Eastern and Gulf Coasts. In Florida, there are several races or subspecies of the Seaside Sparrow, including the "Cape Sable" Seaside Sparrow and the "New Smyrna" Seaside Sparrow, both of which exist in small numbers and are very localized. Another race, the "Dusky" Seaside Sparrow, no longer exists in the wild. Only one male bird remains in captivity at Disney World's Discovery Island.

The Florida Audubon Society is conducting a breeding experiment with the hope of re-introducing the "Dusky" Seaside Sparrow into the wild. Since there are no surviving females, the male will be bred with females of a similar race of Seaside Sparrows. The female offspring will then be crossed back with the surviving "Dusky" male in the hopes of eventually producing offspring that are about 92% "Dusky" Seaside Sparrows.

PS/Vireo

The Sad Fate of the "Dusky"

This is another case of a bird, like the Scrub Jay, that is very restricted in its habitat. It could not survive when that habitat disappeared. The "Dusky" Seaside Sparrow was common on Merritt Island in the 1940's but mosquito control canals changed the habitat as did fires and increased human disturbances. One of the last habitats of the "Dusky" was knowingly destroyed to construct a road at the Kennedy Space Center.

When habitats shrink, birds are crowded together. They become much more vulnerable to disease and to predators. Lack of habitat may restrict feeding and nesting. At some point, the species simply disappears forever.

◁ This is the famous "Dusky" Seaside Sparrow. It is the darkest in color of all the Seaside Sparrows.

Starling

Summer   Winter

EUROPEAN STARLING `YEAR-ROUND`

The starling is one of the most common birds in Florida and may be the most common bird in the entire United States. In 1890, a small flock of starlings was released in New York City. They were part of one man's strange plan to bring to America all the birds mentioned in Shakespeare's plays.* Since then, the starling has proved itself to be one of the most adaptable and resilient bird species known to man.

By prospering to such a degree the starling has made a pest of itself in many ways. Starlings have taken over nesting holes needed to maintain the populations of bluebirds, Tree Swallows, and other birds that nest in cavities. They also take over woodpecker nest holes, but woodpeckers are capable of carving new nests for themselves. Starlings are more of a threat to the cavity-nesting birds that must find nest holes and cannot construct their own.

Starlings love airports and have caused airplane crashes by clogging jet engines with their bodies. In the winter, they travel in huge flocks along with blackbirds and cause problems wherever they decide to roost. Entire woods are made white with their droppings. Tree branches are broken from the weight of so many roosting birds.

*First Part of Henry IV, Act I, Scene III, Line 224.
"But ... I will find him when he lies asleep, and in his ear I'll hollow 'Mortimer.' Nay, I'll have a starling shall be taught to speak nothing but 'Mortimer,' and give it to him to keep his anger still in motion."

△ The starling in summer is black with iridescent blue and green colors. In winter its plumage becomes brightly speckled, and the bird looks strikingly different. The yellow beak seen in summer becomes dark for the winter.

Starling at nest hole

Babies in nest hole

△ A roosting flock of starlings covers a bare tree like leaves. Often such flocks will include large numbers of Red-winged Blackbirds.

This isn't snow!
△ After the starlings and blackbirds leave, the branches are covered with their droppings.

Swallows

Tree Swallow at nest

Migrating flock of Tree Swallows

Nesting Barn Swallows

TREE SWALLOW `WINTER`

Swallows are very similar to swifts, except that they are capable of perching. Although a number of species of swallows migrate through Florida, the swallow that is most frequently seen here is the Tree Swallow. Large flocks of Tree Swallows, sometimes numbering in the tens of thousands, arrive in winter and start devouring wild fruits, especially those of the wax myrtle.

NASA had to remove the wax myrtles at the edge of the Space Shuttle landing strip because they were attracting thousands of Tree Swallows. After gorging themselves, the Tree Swallows would sunbathe on the runway, creating a hazard.

Do the Famous Mission Swallows Really Return on the Same Day?

There is a legend that a flock of Cliff Swallows in California returns to the Mission of El Capistrano on exactly the same day every year. Newspapers nationwide cover the event. The birds do return with regularity, but the idea that they always return on the same day is a myth. The date may vary as much as a week or so either way.

BARN SWALLOW `YEAR-ROUND`

The Barn Swallow is the only swallow in Florida that has a truly forked "swallow tail." The Barn Swallow is also easy to distinguish because it is rust-colored underneath.

Barn Swallows do their feeding away from their nests. For this reason, they defend a very small nesting territory (only as far as they can reach while sitting on the nest).

Barn Swallow

Barn Swallow

Swift

CHIMNEY SWIFT [SUMMER]

The Chimney Swift catches insects in flight. It spends most of its time in the air and even mates without landing. Swifts are indeed very swift and can fly over 100 miles per hour. They generally do not fly this fast because they must make quick turns while hunting their prey.

The Chimney Swift creates its nest with small twigs held together with a special glue manufactured from saliva. The swift's huge saliva glands undergo an enormous enlargement during the breeding season. The nests are usually built in hollow trees, corners of buildings and, as their name implies, inside unused chimneys.

The short, stiff, square tail of the Chimney Swift is used as an extra support for the bird when clinging to walls. The Chimney Swift has sharp claws which are adapted for clinging to a vertical surface and are not very useful for walking. Since perching is not necessary, all four toes are pointed forward for extra clinging ability.

A Rare and Expensive Gourmet Food

Some Asian species of swifts create their nests in large caves and build them entirely of saliva. These nests are the source of a Chinese delicacy, bird's nest soup. This mild-tasting concoction is very expensive. The nests are built very high in rocky caves and can only be gathered by using tall ladders. It is a very difficult and dangerous job. Bird's nest soup is valued for its medicinal properties. It is thought to be a health-giving tonic.

The Prison with No Doors

How does a baby bird escape from its eggshell? Common wisdom has the little fellow "hammering" its way out. But there is no room inside an egg for the bird to swing a hammer (or even a beak). Most baby birds are equipped with an "egg tooth," a projection from the top of the beak which helps weaken the egg through a series of muscular surges by the young bird. It is believed that after the first tiny break in the shell, the hatchling twists around inside the shell and repeats the process until the shell is cut open.

How Birds Are Counted

Bird counts by professionals or skilled amateurs measure the effects of migration on bird populations. But how can you avoid double counting when birds can fly around as the count progresses? During breeding season, birds form territories and tend to stay in them, so counting is not so treacherous. At other times of the year, many species band together to form foraging flocks which travel about in search of food. Double counting is always a danger and the people involved in these counts use care and do the best they can.

47

Tanagers

Male Summer Tanager at nest

SUMMER TANAGER

SUMMER

The Summer Tanager is seen in the United States only in the summer months. It breeds in Florida and other southern states, then spends the winter months in Central and South America.

It is not very common in Florida, but since there are not very many red-colored birds here, it stands out. It is sometimes mistaken for a cardinal, but has no crest and is much more slender. Its feeding habits are similar to those of the fly-catchers. It eats large numbers of insects caught in flight.

SCARLET TANAGER

MIGRANT

The Summer Tanager's beautiful relative, the Scarlet Tanager, is a summer resident of the northeast part of the country and is seen in Florida only during its annual migrations.

Molting is the process by which birds replace old feathers. It usually occurs just before the breeding season in spring when a bird needs to look its best to attract a mate. Some species molt a second time at the close of the breeding season. Birds lose their feathers gradually so that they are never really naked, although some waterbirds become flight-less for a week or so. The photo at far right shows that a bird's coloring can be very different during the molting period.

Female Summer Tanager

The Duller Sex

Why are female birds usually much duller in color than males? Nature has gifted them with much better protective coloration. This camouflage helps them survive when they are confined to the nest during the breeding season. The brightly colored males are better targets for predators.

Scarlet Tanager

Molting Summer Tanager

48

Thrasher

BROWN THRASHER `YEAR-ROUND`

The Brown Thrasher is commonly seen foraging in piles of leaves under oak trees or at the edges of tall grass or scrub plants such as the palmetto. It is sometimes mistaken for a thrush, but it is much larger and its underbody is streaked rather than spotted. It has a distinctively long tail and a beautiful yellow eye.

The Brown Thrasher is closely related to the mockingbird, and except for the color, the resemblance is clear. Note the long tail, the beak, the general size and shape. Also, like the mockingbird, the Brown Thrasher is a skilled singer.

Count the Verses
The mockingbird usually repeats its calls six times or more, the Brown Thrasher in groups of two.

The Meaning of "Rufous"
If you are not yet a birder, you may think "rufous" is a character in the Gasoline Alley comic strip (actually, that fellow's name is spelled "Rufus"). But "rufous" refers to a certain reddish-brown color. The word is sometimes used by artists and for some reason is used with great frequency in describing birds. The back of the Brown Thrasher is a good example of this special color.

Bird Songs
Many birds have a range of four octaves and have the amazing ability to sing several notes at the same time. This fact was determined by scientific instruments. The simultaneous notes cannot be distinguished by the human ear.

Many bird sounds which are not pleasing to us may be composed of hundreds of rapid notes which seem blurred together into a buzz because of our inability to distinguish the individual sounds.

Birds sing to mark territories and attract mates. Their vocal equipment is vastly more sophisticated than our own and they clearly use it to communicate. Apparently, it is only brain power that limits them from developing a full-fledged language.

Keeping Score at Your Feeder
By observing and recording which birds are chased away from your feeder and by which species, you can determine a general pecking order for your backyard. Not every feeder will be the same, and the pecking order may change with the seasons. Also, hunger may make an individual bird far more aggressive and completely upset the normal pecking order.

Thrushes

WOOD THRUSH

None of the thrushes are common in Florida. These birds are smaller than the similar Brown Thrasher. Also, their breasts are dotted rather than streaked and they are chunkier birds.

Many thrush nests are found in Christmas trees that are shipped from the North for sale in Florida.

All of the thrushes in Florida are look-alikes. But even though their plumage is similar, their songs are very different.

SWAINSON'S THRUSH

Note the buff-colored eye-ring which distinguishes this bird from other thrushes.

GRAY-CHEEKED THRUSH

▽ This thrush is common along the Gulf Coast during spring migration, but rare during fall migration because these birds take a different route (through Texas) in the fall.

Wood Thrush

Swainson's Thrush

What Does "Species" mean?

The definition of "species" has changed through the years, and it is still difficult at times for ornithologists to decide how to classify a certain bird. That is why bird names are sometimes changed as new information appears. It is also why birds within a species are sometimes further divided into "subspecies" (also called "races" or "tribes").

At first, ornithologists depended upon similarities in appearance. The next standard was whether the bird could breed in the wild and produce viable offspring. At one time, even song patterns were considered in classification. The latest approach involves the study of similarities in DNA structure.

Bird watchers are sometimes annoyed when species are changed, because if two species are combined, it may reduce the number of birds on their lists. But advances in scientific knowledge require that classifications be updated once in a while.

I Wish I May, I Wish I Mite

If every little birdie had its wish, those pesky feather mites would disappear for good. But, every bird has them, and they make a fascinating study in themselves.

Mites are arachnids (tiny creatures related to spiders). They live on birds and eat the feathers and flakes of skin. Birds have other parasites such as feather lice which do much the same things. Dust baths, sunbathing, and anting (see page 30) are ways in which birds try to alleviate this problem.

Titmouse

TUFTED TITMOUSE [YEAR-ROUND]

The titmouse is considered a leader of the "mixed flocks" of small birds that gather in the winter. Its song sounds like "Peter, Peter, Peter."

The Fine Art of Pishing

It may sound a little vulgar, but "pishing" is what birders call the "Pshhhhhh, Pshhhhhh, Pshhhhhh" sound they make to attract those little birds (such as titmice) who ordinarily stay hidden. This noise sounds like another bird scolding a predator, such as an owl. They all quickly come to investigate. If a real owl were discovered, a group of the small birds would gang up to harass him and chase him away. Playing a tape recorded owl call will also attract the same little birds, but "pishing" is much more convenient.

Towhee

RUFOUS-SIDED TOWHEE [YEAR-ROUND]

The towhee says its name. In the North it is also called the "chewink," a name which sounds like another one of the towhee's calls. Some Floridians think the call sounds like "jo-ree", and so it earns yet another name.

The towhee has interesting feeding habits. It forages along the ground in brush piles, leaves and heavy underbrush. It kicks backwards with both feet at the same time to rake away leaves and expose seeds and insects on the ground. It is one of only a few birds in the world to use this double kicking method of foraging.

Female Towhee

Male

Male

In Florida, most towhees (except for the migrants) have light-coloured eyes. Towhees from the northern states have red eyes. Eye color can vary, but in general, the farther north the towhee, the redder the eye.

The red-eyed birds and the white-eyed birds used to be considered separate species, but long ago it was learned that they could interbreed, so now they are grouped together.

Turkey

WILD TURKEY

The Spanish explorers were very much impressed with this bird and took some breeding specimens back to Europe. This species was a common game animal in America in Pilgrim times and later was nearly driven to extinction by overhunting. It is now making a strong comeback throughout Florida and many other states.

In contrast to the domestic turkey, hunters consider the Wild Turkey a very alert and challenging prey. This bird's contributions to the survival of the early settlers caused Benjamin Franklin to suggest its use as the national symbol. He considered it a far "nobler" bird than the Bald Eagle which, he noted, steals food from other birds and eats dead animals.

The male turkey has a large tail which it can spread in a fan-shaped display like a peacock. Mature males also have a tuft of feathers extending from the breast which is called a "beard." Male turkeys have a hind toe raised off the ground called a "spur." Female turkeys are called "hens," young males "jakes," and mature males "gobblers."

Male and female

White Meat of Turkey

Dark meat is common in the breasts of birds that fly long distances. The dark color is caused by the abundant blood vessels needed to sustain long flight. Domestic turkeys that can't fly far have white breast meat but dark leg meat due to their constant walking.

Male turkeys have large, fleshy growths on their heads called "caruncles." These growths have a decorative function and become more brightly colored during mating displays. Similar growths are found on other birds. If they appear on the top of the head (like a rooster), they are "combs." If they hang below the head, they are "wattles."

Gang Wars

Turkey families fight as a group. The dominant brother will take on rivals from other families and is backed up by his other brothers. These gangs are called "sib-ship" groups.

Vireos

Vireo means "I am green" in Latin. Most of the species of Vireos do have some form of green coloring, usually a dull olive green. Another interesting feature of these small songbirds is the tiny hook at the tip of the upper bill.

Vireos catch insects but also eat berries such as those of the wax myrtle and even the fruit of the poison ivy vine.

Vireos sing beautiful songs, but they tend to stay hidden in foliage. They are well camouflaged and not as active as many of the other small birds.

WHITE-EYED VIREO   `YEAR-ROUND`

▷ The White-eyed Vireo and the Solitary Vireo are members of a group of vireos that have eye-rings and white stripes on their wings (called "wingbars").

Another group of vireos including the Red-eyed Vireo and the Black-whiskered Vireo have eye-stripes rather than eye-rings and lack the wing-bars.

Red-eyed Vireos sing all the time during breeding season and have been observed singing thousands of verses in a single day.

SOLITARY VIREO   `WINTER`

◁ The Solitary Vireo is noted for its blue-gray head color and its white eye-ring. The Solitary's eye-ring extends around the beak. Birders call this type of marking "spectacles."

RED-EYED VIREO   `SUMMER`

△ The Red-eyed Vireo has an eye which may be a bit red, but it sometimes strains the imagination to actually see the red color.

BLACK-WHISKERED VIREO   `SUMMER`

▷ The Black-whiskered Vireo is common in the Florida keys. The black streak under the eye is called a "whisker."

Whip-poor-will

AND OTHER NIGHTJARS

Whip-poor-will

There are three types of nightjars in Florida and they all look remarkably similar except for some small size differences.

WHIP-POOR-WILL WINTER

The Whip-poor-will is a member of a group of birds known as nightjars or goatsuckers. The name "nightjar" refers to their tendency to disturb the night with their calls.

The name "goatsucker" derives from an ancient belief that these birds milked the udders of goats for nourishment and that the goats sometimes went blind as a consequence.

CHUCK-WILLS-WIDOW SUMMER

The "WHIP-poor-WILL" sound is a very common nighttime cry in undeveloped parts of the state. Most people just assume the sound is coming from the familiar Whip-poor-will. But this species is only here briefly during the early spring migration.

The sound in summer is probably made by a Chuck-wills-widow, a summer resident. The cry of this bird is very similar to that of the Whip-poorwill, but if you are close enough you will hear that each verse is preceded by a soft "chuck" sound.

◁△▽ The Chuck-wills-widow is larger and more brownish than the very similar Whip-poor-will. Note the whiskers which help funnel insects into the large mouth during flight.

54

COMMON NIGHTHAWK

Nighthawks can sometimes be spotted on a tree branch, in ground-cover, or on a stump or fence. In spite of their superb camouflage and their ability to sit motionless, a lucky birder walking through a wooded area will occasionally get a glimpse.

Nighthawks eat mostly insects, especially moths, and are well equipped for the job with huge, scoop-like mouths. Surrounding their mouths are long whiskers which help funnel insect prey into the mouth opening.

It is believed that some nightjars have a sonar system, like bats, which helps to locate prey in the dark, and also helps avoid collisions with trees during night flights.

Common Nighthawk

The Common Nighthawk hunts insects on the wing and is easily recognized by the white marking under each wing. If you are driving along a country road at dusk or at night and see a rapidly moving bird with a white mark on each wing criss-crossing the road, it is most likely a nighthawk. They often hunt over roads. Among rural Floridians, this bird is called a "bullbat," because of its bat-like feeding behavior.

Nighthawks are not hawks despite their name. Among other important differences, they lack the strong talons that are common to these birds of prey. Since nighthawks hunt insects by scooping them up with their mouths, they have no need for strong claws.

Nighthawks often nest on the roofs of buildings. Other Florida birds found nesting on roofs include the Killdeer and the Least Tern.

△ These nighthawks are perched in a "protective crouch" which helps them take full advantage of their camouflage to blend with a branch or fence.

▷ In flight the Common Nighthawk shows a white bar on each wing which is very handy for identification.

◁ Nighthawk on the ground shows a "threat display" to an intruder.

Wood Warblers

Warblers are one of the most colorful and varied groups of birds and for this reason, stir a lot of interest among birders. Roger Tory Peterson, author of the most famous bird field guide series, calls them the "butterflies of the bird world."

They are found exclusively in the New World (western hemisphere). There are fifty-three different species of Wood Warblers in the United States and Canada. Most of them can be seen in Florida during migration.

Warblers are tiny birds with sharp-pointed bills. Most of them have some areas of yellow coloring. Their food consists largely of insects taken from the crevices of tree trunks and tree limbs. Most do eat some fruit. The Ovenbird is a bit different. It forages on the ground like a thrush.

Most warblers do not warble in the sense of singing musical notes. They make a variety of sounds including hisses, buzzes, screeches, and whistles.

COMMON YELLOW-THROAT
`YEAR-ROUND`

△ This is one of the warblers most commonly seen in Florida. It is found in marshes and is easily recognized by its black "Lone Ranger" face mask.

AMERICAN REDSTART
`WINTER`

▽ This bird has the interesting habit of fanning its tail wide open as it chases insects, flitting around like a butterfly.

Cape May Warbler

CAPE MAY WARBLER
 `MIGRANT`

△ This Cape May Warbler is perched in a bottlebrush, one of the many beautiful flowering trees of South Florida. This warbler also likes the silk-oak trees because they attract a lot of insects to their flowers. The Cape May Warblers migrate in masses, so you might see a dozen or two dozen of these birds in a single tree.

OVENBIRD
`MIGRANT`

▷ The Ovenbird is a migrant but one of the most common warblers seen in the Everglades. The Ovenbird lives on the ground and depends heavily on camouflage. It frequently will remain motionless until an intruder almost steps on it, taking off only at the last second.

Wood Warblers

Northern Parula Warbler

More about Warblers

Although some warblers are year-round residents in Florida, many species breed in the northern United States and Canada. The breeding season lasts for about three months, then they spend several months in migration, and about six months wintering in Central and South America. There is a theory that these birds are basically South American species that developed the migratory habit of breeding in North America because it allowed them to escape competition from other local species during this important period.

Warblers are night fliers during migration and encounter tremendous losses during their journeys. One big hazard for these birds has been television towers with long guy wires. One television tower in Florida killed thousands of migratory birds in a single season. Most of these birds were warblers.

NORTHERN PARULA WARBLER
[MIGRANT]

This is a bird of the deep woods so it is seldom seen. But it is a common breeding bird in Florida, and it uses spanish moss to build its nest. The name of this species is pronounced "pear-ou-lah."

BLACK AND WHITE WARBLER
[WINTER]

▷ This is a fairly common backyard bird. Its behavior is a little different from other warblers. It walks around tree limbs looking for insects and is most commonly seen in an upside-down position.

Black and White Warbler

Whiplash from Warblers

Birders should consider a good insurance policy before going after these birds because it is easy to strain the neck watching them dash around in the upper branches of trees.

PROTHONOTARY WARBLER
[MIGRANT]

△ The name "Prothonotary" comes from "Protonotary," an official of the Roman Catholic Church whose function is to keep records of certain acts of the Pope and whose official regalia includes a bright yellow hood.

PALM WARBLER
[WINTER]

△ The Palm Warbler is often seen in saw palmettos. This bird is one of a number of birds known to be "tail-waggers."

BLACK-THROATED BLUE WARBLER
[MIGRANT]

△ This warbler is one of the least shy of all warblers. It is frequently seen in backyards, parks, and other suburban surroundings.

Wood Warblers

Yellow-rumped (Winter)

YELLOW-RUMPED WARBLER `WINTER`

△▽Almost every yard in the state has hosted this warbler at one time or another. Unfortunately, when passing through Florida, it is usually seen in its drab winter plumage (as shown in photo below). It is one of the warbler species most commonly seen during migration in spring and fall.

Yellow-Rumped Warbler (winter plumage)

CHESTNUT-SIDED WARBLER `MIGRANT`

△ This is the only warbler with an all white throat, breast, and belly. Note the brown (chestnut) colored stripe on its side visible just under the wing.

ORANGE-CROWNED WARBLER `MIGRANT`

◁ This little bird is quite dull compared to many other warblers. It does have a touch of orange on its head, but these feathers are only seen when the bird is excited.

PINE WARBLER `YEAR-ROUND`

△ Although the Pine Warbler has one of the prettiest songs, it usually stays high up in tall pine trees and is seldom seen.

HOODED WARBLER `MIGRANT`

△ The black hood of the male Hooded Warbler is like a monk's cowl, covering the top of the head and circling the face.

Birding Activities

What do "birders" do in the pursuit of their hobby? Many are "listers." They keep lists of all the species of birds they have personally observed and identified. For some people this is a very competitive activity. There are state lists (birds seen in one's own state), "life lists" (a total of all birds seen anywhere), North American lists, etc. After all the common and uncommon birds have been sighted, the really competitive part becomes a matter of spotting the rare appearances of birds that are out of their normal range. These birds are called "accidentals" or "vagrants."

The birding community is very enthusiastic (some would say fanatic).

Doonesbury BY GARRY TRUDEAU

The sighting of a rare accidental often excites hundreds of people to board airplanes and travel long distances to add to their lists. This is called "blitzing" among the faithful. Some birders pay a fee to subscribe to a hotline service which alerts them to these opportunities. Really hotshot listers have North American lists of over 600 species.

Birders also compete for the most birds seen in a single year. It helps to be rich because top competitors must fly all over the country and immediately zoom to any place where a rare bird has been spotted. The record for a one-year list is 713 species, far more than most birders have on their life lists.

A Question of Residency

In this book birds, are described as year-round residents, summer residents, winter residents, or migrants "just passing through" who stop only briefly to refuel. But this is a simplification. Residency is quite a complicated issue. A number of "summer residents" can be found remaining in extreme South Florida during the winter. Some birds that live here in small numbers year-round are scarcely noticed until the large migratory flocks arrive. The labels used in this book are only given as a general guide to suggest when to look for certain birds.

Here is the normal migratory pattern. Most migratory birds nest in the northern states or Canada during summer and fly south to Florida and South America for the winter. Migratory flocks pass through Florida again in the spring as they return to their nesting grounds in the north.

But Florida is also host to some birds from South America who fly north to Florida for nesting in the summer. We are at the top of the range instead of the bottom for these birds. For this reason, some of the birds that nest in Florida are only summer residents, rather than permanent residents.

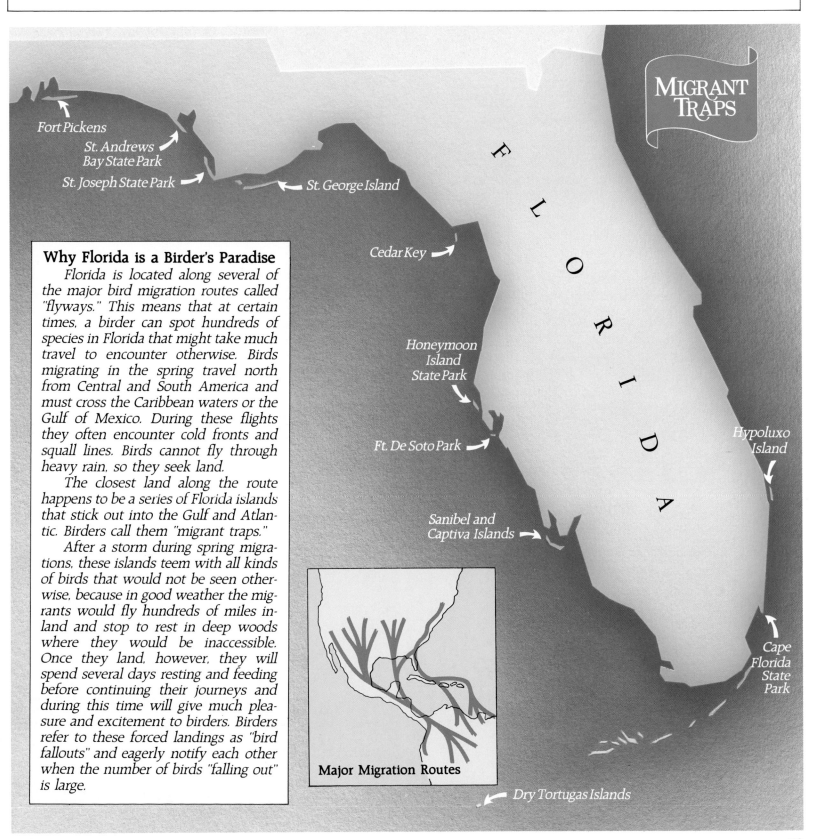

MIGRANT TRAPS

Fort Pickens
St. Andrews Bay State Park
St. Joseph State Park
St. George Island
Cedar Key

FLORIDA

Honeymoon Island State Park
Ft. De Soto Park
Sanibel and Captiva Islands
Hypoluxo Island
Cape Florida State Park
Dry Tortugas Islands

Major Migration Routes

Why Florida is a Birder's Paradise

Florida is located along several of the major bird migration routes called "flyways." This means that at certain times, a birder can spot hundreds of species in Florida that might take much travel to encounter otherwise. Birds migrating in the spring travel north from Central and South America and must cross the Caribbean waters or the Gulf of Mexico. During these flights they often encounter cold fronts and squall lines. Birds cannot fly through heavy rain, so they seek land.

The closest land along the route happens to be a series of Florida islands that stick out into the Gulf and Atlantic. Birders call them "migrant traps."

After a storm during spring migrations, these islands teem with all kinds of birds that would not be seen otherwise, because in good weather the migrants would fly hundreds of miles inland and stop to rest in deep woods where they would be inaccessible. Once they land, however, they will spend several days resting and feeding before continuing their journeys and during this time will give much pleasure and excitement to birders. Birders refer to these forced landings as "bird fallouts" and eagerly notify each other when the number of birds "falling out" is large.

Waxwing

CEDAR WAXWING

The Cedar Waxwing's face mask and crest makes it very distinctive. Also impressive is the size of the waxwing flocks which arrive in Florida in the winter to eat fruits and berries from Florida plants such as the pyracantha. Cedar Waxwings rely heavily on berries. In turn, they are important in dispersing the seeds contained in these fruits. Flocks of these birds can strip a holly tree in just a few minutes.

Once recognized, the Cedar Waxwing's call, a high-pitched "zeee" sound, is unmistakable and often can be distinguished as large flocks of migrating birds fly overhead.

Waxwings are known for an especially interesting act of cooperative behavior. A group of birds sitting on a branch will pass berries from one bird to another down the line until all have been fed.

Waxwings are very social and not only migrate in flocks but stay together in groups in the areas where they nest.

▷ The name "waxwing" comes from the brilliant red tips of the wing feathers which look like drops of bright red candle wax.

Woodcock

AMERICAN WOODCOCK [WINTER]

Woodcocks, also known as "timberdoodles," are hard to distinguish from Snipes. Snipes are common here in winter, but woodcocks are rare birds in much of Florida. They prefer heavy woods near water where they probe the ground for worms much like the Snipe.

There is a Woodcock National Wildlife Refuge near Eastport, Maine, but even there they are hard to find. The reason is that they stay hidden and are perfectly camouflaged.

Woodcocks have amazing peripheral vision. Their somewhat bug-eyed appearance is due to the wide placement of their eyes on the sides of their heads.

△ "Going to town on a Saturday night." An American Woodcock makes a rare visit to civilization.

Miscellaneous Migrants

Covering all the migrant birds that can be seen in Florida would be beyond the scope of this book. A complete list would include hundreds of species. Here are just a few more of the many beautiful migrants which can be spotted if you are lucky.

Evening Grosbeak

Bobolink

Rose-Breasted Grosbeak

Blue Grosbeak

Woodpeckers

Woodpeckers are very important for control of wood-boring insects, and their effect is magnified because, after a woodpecker has opened the bark, other birds can also hunt the insects inside. But, improved forestry techniques along with man's development of many woodland areas has meant less dead trees for nesting and feeding and a decline of woodpecker populations. Competition from starlings for nesting sites has added to the problem.

Many woodpeckers have stiff tail feathers which, like those of the Chimney Swift, help brace the birds as they cling vertically to trees.

RED-BELLIED WOODPECKER `YEAR-ROUND`

This is the most common woodpecker in Florida. It can be remarkably tame at times. It is a member of a group of woodpeckers called "ladderbacks," because of the step-by-step black and white pattern on its back.

In spite of its name, its belly is rather white. If you look closely, there is just a touch of reddish color on the belly. It is sometimes visible if the bird is in just the right position. This reddish patch becomes much more prominent during the breeding season (March to August).

The Red-bellied Woodpecker is often confused with the Red-headed Woodpecker because both have red markings on their heads. But the Red-bellied Woodpecker only has a stripe of red on top; its head is not entirely red. This bird is frequently seen in dead palm trees and also in oak trees where it eats acorns in addition to insects.

Male
Red-bellied
Woodpecker

△ Red-bellied Woodpecker finally shows his red belly — such as it is.

◁ The beautiful "ladder-backed" pattern is prominent on this juvenile Red-bellied Woodpecker, but he does not yet have the distinctive red stripe on his head.

DOWNY WOODPECKER YEAR-ROUND

The downy is the smallest woodpecker in Florida. It is often seen at suet feeders in the winter.

When freezes kill orange trees, the dead trees are often used as nest sites by downies.

Female

△ Upside down downy? This little woodpecker is frequently seen in this position. Notice the white patch on its back.

▷ The male downy has a small red patch on the back of its head.

◁ The female looks very much like the male, but does not have the red patch.

Male

Why Do Woodpeckers Pound on Trees?

Their beating and chiseling helps them find food by removing bark and revealing hidden insects. It allows them to carve nesting cavities. Their pounding creates a drum-beat rhythm that substitutes for song and will attract a mate, or alert other males to a territorial claim. Woodpeckers have been observed drumming when there was no apparent purpose. There is speculation that they sometimes pound just for the pure joy of the sound, but this has not been proven.

Why Do Woodpeckers Pound on Wooden Houses?

They are usually looking for food or sounding to mark their territories. It could be an indication that a building has termites. In one case it was determined that a woodpecker was drilling the side of a house because of the ticking of an alarm clock inside. Woodpeckers often locate insects by sound, so the ticking noise caught the bird's attention.

This Hairy Woodpecker just caught a mouthful of ants.

HAIRY WOODPECKER YEAR-ROUND

This woodpecker looks like a large Downy Woodpecker, but has a much longer beak. It is a seldom-seen resident of the deep woods, swamps and old growth pine forests.

Woodpeckers

COMMON FLICKER (YELLOW-SHAFTED)

`YEAR-ROUND`

There are two types of flickers in the United States. One in the west has a reddish color under its wing and tail feathers and is called Red-shafted. The flicker found in Florida shows bright yellow under the wing and tail feathers and is called Yellow-shafted.

This woodpecker is often seen on the ground where it hunts for ants and eats berries. It is different from most of the other Florida woodpeckers because its back is brownish in color rather than having a black and white pattern. When the bird flies away, it shows a white patch on its rump.

The adult flicker has a red "V" shaped marking on the back of its head. The male also has a black stripe extending downward from its beak. Birders call it a "moustache." It is technically called a "malar stripe."

▷ This flicker shows a trace of the yellow-shafted wing feathers. This view also reveals the red "V" shaped marking on the back of the neck.

△ Flicker on the ground hunting ants.

△ The female is similar to the male, but lacks the black "moustache" marking.

PILEATED WOODPECKER   (YEAR-ROUND)

This is the largest Florida woodpecker. Its enormous size and flashy red tuft of feathers on its head mark it as a most impressive bird.

Pileated Woodpeckers have very powerful bills. When they start to chisel, the chips really fly and not small chips either. They are capable of getting to insect colonies deep inside trees. Partially rotted logs of considerable size can be completely demolished in very little time.

Cavities in trees created by Pileated Woodpeckers just for sleeping are large and the holes are usually oblong rather than round. These are called "bedroom nests." The holes of nesting cavities used for breeding are usually more roundish in shape.

Some people pronounce the name PILL-ee-ated and some pronounce it PIE-lee-ated. Both ways are acceptable. It depends on whether you choose to use the Latinized pronunciation or the English pronunciation.

Female

Male

Woodpecker Wives Must Use Some Other Excuse

Woodpeckers are headache-proof. Their bills do not connect directly to their skulls. There is shock-absorbing tissue in between that allows them to pound for hours every day without taking any aspirin. Woodpeckers can strike hard wood at the rate of more than ten times per second. The ability of this tissue to spring back to shape and cushion again between each strike compares favorably with the best man-made shock-absorbing materials.

Male and female are very similar, but the female has a black forehead and lacks the small red mark of the male which appears below the eye.

Another difference between male and female Pileated Woodpeackers is that the male has an additional red marking beneath the beak (called a "moustache" by birders).

Woodpeckers

YELLOW-BELLIED SAPSUCKER [WINTER]

This woodpecker earns its living by drilling many rows of small holes in a tree's trunk, then returning to lick up the sap that drips from these open wounds. The sap attracts insects which provide additional food.

RED-COCKADED WOODPECKER [YEAR-ROUND]

This small woodpecker is quite rare and endangered. "Cockade" means a small ribbon decoration worn on a hat but is used in this case to refer to the tiny spot of red color just behind the eye of the male. There are small populations of Red-cockaded Woodpeckers still surviving in several areas of Florida. Development projects in these areas have been delayed and modified to prevent extinction of this bird.

The Red-cockaded Woodpecker always constructs its nest in a living pine tree. Other woodpeckers drill nests in dead trees whenever possible because it is easier. The Red-cockaded Woodpecker requires very old pines that are infected with heart rot (red-heart fungus). This very specialized requirement for nesting sites is the cause of the decline of the species, since logging has removed much of its nesting habitat and forests are being replanted with a longleaf pine that does not get red-heart fungus.

The Red-cockaded Woodpecker drills a series of holes around the nest cavity. Large amounts of sap flow from these holes. Their nests are easily spotted because of the white streaks of sap on the bark of the tree. The sticky sap helps protect the nest from predators such as snakes.

RED-HEADED WOODPECKER [YEAR-ROUND]

Although many woodpeckers have red markings on the head, this is the only woodpecker whose head is solid red in color. This species is not very common in Florida, but is frequently seen around Rollins College in winter.

IVORY-BILLED WOODPECKER

Last seen in Florida in 1969, the Ivory-billed Woodpecker may be extinct, but nobody knows for sure. There have been confirmed sightings in Cuba in 1986 of a subspecies called the Zapata Ivory-billed and occasional unconfirmed reports in Florida, South Carolina, and Louisiana. The Ivory-billed is often confused with the Pileated Woodpecker but is larger, with a white bill and white tips on its wing-feathers.

Long ago Ivory-billed Woodpeckers were plentiful. The American Indians made necklaces of their beaks and the pioneers made pouches of their scalps. The demise of these birds is linked to excessive lumbering, which destroyed much of their habitat, and over-hunting.

Audubon Did It Too

In many bird books written thirty or forty years ago, there is constant reference to "collecting" specimens, which basically meant killing the birds for further study or for display as mounted specimens. Today, most ornithologists opt for collecting with a camera, especially with rare species, although a certain number of skins are still taken with proper government permits.

Watercolor © 1986 Ernest C. Simmons

Wrens

CAROLINA WREN

YEAR-ROUND

The Carolina Wren is the most common wren in Florida. It is quite comfortable around man and has the endearing habit of nesting in all kinds of man-made containers, from flower pots to an old apron. Many people have laid down some object, such as an old hat, in a garage and later found they could not use the item until a pair of wrens had finished their nesting season.

The Carolina Wren has a very loud song for its size. Wrens are insect-eaters and are regarded as very beneficial to man.

Nesting Territories

When it comes to defending a nest, most birds are only worried about their own kind. This is why several different species of birds may nest in the same tree without any problem.

More Details about Breeding

A common feature of migratory species is that the males will arrive in a breeding area first and establish territories. The females will arrive a week or so later and the males will be ready to start competing for mates.

SEDGE WREN

WINTER

This shy bird was formerly called the Short-billed Marsh Wren. The male perches in tall grasses to sing and may sing at night. The Sedge Wren does not like its habitat to be too wet and is more likely to be found in meadows than in reeds and cattails.

What Makes a Male Bird Sexy?

For many species, the female's preferences are an important part of mating. It is not completely known what factors female birds consider in choosing mates. It may be that the quality of the male's territory is the main factor. In other words, they marry for money. Male aggressiveness, and a strong, clear, song may be important in attracting a female, but on the other hand, the stronger birds will most likely also have the best territories. Sometimes a female will choose to share a mated male who possesses a fine territory rather than choose an unmated male with a lesser territory.

HOUSE WREN

WINTER

The House Wren is quite common in Florida during the winter. These wrens have been described as "mouse-like" because they often prefer to run through the grasses rather than fly.

Sedge Wren

House Wren

The Big Three

In the common Florida habitat called "pine flatwoods," where there is a mixture of pine trees and scrub palmetto, three of the most common birds are the Carolina Wren, the Rufous-sided Towhee, and the Common Yellow-throat.

Birds of prey, also known as "raptors" (from a Latin word meaning to rob, seize, and carry off), kill other animals for food. In American Indian cultures, these birds were admired and even worshipped for their hunting skills. The early European settlers saw these same birds occasionally kill domestic animals and viewed them as a threat to survival. It is theorized that from this history, fear and hatred of birds of prey was passed down through the generations. Certainly it is felt by some people today.

It is now known that predators and their prey are dependent upon each other. If predators do not hold populations of prey animals in check, these animals might overpopulate and destroy their food supply, thereby threatening their own survival. If the population of the prey animals declines, so will the population of predators, so a balance of both populations is maintained.

Caracara

CRESTED CARACARA

YEAR-ROUND

This fascinating bird of prey is found on the prairies of central Florida where its habitat is maintained on some of the vast cattle ranches between Orlando and Lake Okeechobee. It is a member of the falcon family and is sometimes called the Mexican Eagle. Its image is found on Mexican coins.

The small numbers of caracaras living in Florida (perhaps fewer than 500 birds) are very isolated from the main populations in Central and South America. They are slightly different from those birds and are classified as a subspecies called "Audubon's Caracara."

The caracara usually sits on a high perch and flies out to capture prey, but can forage on the ground also. Its diet is more varied than that of any other bird of prey. It will eat any creature that it can manage to overpower. It has even been observed swallowing baby alligators! The caracara is as ferocious as it looks and has been known to chase Bald Eagles away from kills.

A Story from the Ice Age

At the end of the Ice Age a million years ago, the polar ice cap began to melt and sea levels rose creating the Gulf of Mexico and dividing Florida from Mexico. This also divided the populations of a number of animals such as the Burrowing Owl, the Scrub Jay, and the Crested Caracara, all of whom still have relatives living in Mexico and the American West. As a result of small adaptations and changes during centuries of isolation, many of those creatures left in Florida are now sufficiently different to be classified as "subspecies."

Eagle

Eagle

BALD EAGLE

WINTER

Florida is an excellent place to observe the national bird. Next to Alaska, Florida has the most breeding pairs of any state. The Eagle is endangered, with probably less than 500 pairs remaining in the lower 48 states.

Bald Eagles are not bald. The adult birds (male and female) have white feathers on their heads. The young birds have dark heads and do not get their white heads and tail feathers until they are three to five years old.

There are northern and southern subspecies of the Bald Eagle. The main difference is that the northern Bald Eagle is slightly larger. Sometimes, when northern eagles have migrated into this area, they can be seen sitting next to southern eagles and the size difference (which some people might mistakenly attribute to an age difference) is apparent.

Size differences can be misleading because there is a difference in size between male and female eagles. As with most other raptors, the female bird is larger.

Bald Eagles have a spectacular courtship ritual known as a "cartwheel display" in which the male and female eagles grasp each other's talons and tumble over and over through the sky.

△ Close-up photo shows details of white head-feathers.

△ Immature Bald Eagles are dark in color.

NASA Focuses on the National Bird

Eagles build huge nests and return to them year after year The nest shown is seven feet wide and 60 feet above the ground. It was constructed at the Kennedy Space Center. Surplus land at the center is maintained by the US Wildlife Service to preserve habitat for Florida birds and animals. The nesting photos were taken by NASA photographers with a remote controlled camera placed in a weather-proof box only a few feet from the nest.

◁ Before laying eggs, the eagles prepared the nest by collecting branches. The branches were used to build a barrier around the edge of the nest. Through such annual additions, eagle nests keep growing in size each year until they are destroyed by storms. Sometimes they survive for many years and become truly huge structures. The one shown in these photos is over 20 years old.

▷ Eagles usually nest in tall pines near water. Their diet includes a lot of fish and some waterfowl such as coots and moorhen. Fish can be caught by grabbing them out of the water with their talons, or by stealing them from Ospreys, but the Bald Eagle is a carrion-eater and the bulk of its diet is dead fish.

◁ The down-covered chick is only a few inches long at birth, but growth is fast. The young eagle will be flying in a couple of months.

▷ Note the dark plumage of the young bird. This eaglet was observed preparing for his first flight. First he extended and flapped his wings, then he began a series of bounces and jumps, rising higher from the nest each time until he could rise several feet into the air and was ready for actual flight.

This nesting began in the fall, and by March the eaglets had hatched, learned to fly and find food, and had left the nest.

In summer the young eagles disperse from Florida to the northern states.

Falcons

AMERICAN KESTREL

WINTER

Also known as "sparrow hawks," kestrels reside in Florida all year but their population greatly increases with the addition of winter migrants.

The name "sparrow hawk" is not really appropriate because this bird feeds primarily on insects, and also lizards. It requires a high perch for spotting its prey. It is usually seen in the open countryside perched on the limb of a tree and is frequently seen on phone wires.

"Eyes" in the Back of the Head

The kestrel has two spots on the back of its head. It is theorized that these spots resemble eyes from a distance. They may help prevent attacks from the rear by larger raptors by giving the illusion that the kestrel is facing the attacker and therefore is less likely to be taken by surprise.

PEREGRINE FALCON

The Peregrine Falcon nearly became extinct as it suffered the harsh effects of pesticides in the environment. Thanks to efforts by the Cornell University Laboratory of Ornithology, captive breeding of this species produced enough birds for release in the wild to restore populations in areas where they had fallen dangerously.

Centuries ago, the Peregrine Falcon was used by Arabs along the Persian Gulf to hunt for food. Falconry is still very popular in that region as a sport. Top quality birds captured in the wild (so that they do not have to be taught to hunt) can bring prices up to $100,000. This means that smuggling birds can be as profitable as smuggling drugs. It has put extra pressure on the Peregrine Falcon populations in spite of law enforcement efforts.

The Peregrine Falcon dives on its prey at enormous speeds variously estimated from 100 miles per hour to more than twice that speed. A Peregrine Falcon kills its prey by striking it hard with a foot balled-up like a fist or by grasping it with sharp talons.

The Peregrine Falcon usually nests on rocky cliffs overlooking water and has been known on rare occasions to nest on high-rise office buildings in big cities. In Florida, the Peregrine Falcon does not nest, but it is seen in migration, especially in the Miami area. A few remain during the winter. They are most frequently seen along the beaches and mud flats where potential prey such as shorebirds and waterfowl congregate.

Sport falconry exists in this country, but there are not many practitioners. It takes a great deal of effort. The trainer and the bird must work together daily.

△ Elaborate headgear is used in sport falconry.

△ Peregrine Falcon showing the pointed wings that are typical of most falcons.

▷ Female Merlins are brown in color.

MERLIN

The Merlin is midway in size between the tiny American Kestrel and the much larger Peregrine Falcon. The male Merlin has gray-colored wings like the Peregrine Falcon. Formerly, the Merlin was known as the Pigeon Hawk. Merlins are not common in Florida but can be seen during migration, especially along the beaches.

Hawks

RED-TAILED HAWK

YEAR-ROUND

Of all the hawks, the red-tailed are the most widespread in the United States.

◁ This view shows the reddish colored tail-feathers which give this hawk its name. Only the mature birds have the red tail.

△ A Red-tailed Hawk at its nest with downy chicks. Red-tailed Hawks have a white breast with a band of streaks across the belly that birders call a "cummerbund."

SHARP-SHINNED HAWK WINTER

Known as a "sharpie" among birders, this small hawk is responsible for most of the bird kills around backyard feeders. Sharpies will find a perch in view of a feeder and wait until small birds appear before striking.

If you notice this happening in your yard, remove the food from the feeder and don't feed the birds for several days. The sharpie will get tired of waiting and move on. With good hunting, the sharpie may stay near your feeder for months. Planting dense shrubbery near the feeder will provide the birds with some protective cover.

On the other hand, there are some people who would much prefer the hawk and wouldn't mind losing a few song birds to keep him around.

Sharp-shinned Hawk

Note the difference in the length of the tail feathers between the "Sharpie" and the rare Short-tailed Hawk.

COOPER'S HAWK YEAR-ROUND

△ Cooper's Hawk is almost identical to the Sharp-shinned Hawk. It is larger and its tail is rounded rather than square, but it may be impossible to tell the difference by casual observation.

SHORT-TAILED HAWK YEAR-ROUND

◁ The Short-tailed Hawk is seen in two color forms; the light phase is white underneath and the dark phase is black underneath. It is rather rare in Florida, but is easily recognized in flight because it is the only Florida hawk whose underside is all white or all black.

The Short-tailed Hawk's small population is concentrated in the southern part of the state. The best place to look for this bird is the Big Cypress Swamp and the Everglades during winter. Fish Eating Creek is an especially good location.

Short-tailed Hawk

RED-SHOULDERED HAWK YEAR-ROUND

Note the patch of reddish color on the shoulder. These hawks are found in wet areas near streams and swamps unlike the Red-tailed Hawk which prefers drier woodlands.

△ Note that the Red-shouldered Hawks found in South Florida are quite pale in color compared to those found further north.

The Red-shouldered Hawk has a very interesting courtship display. A pair of Red-shouldered Hawks will roll over on their backs during flight and may even fly upside down for a short distance. They are known to decorate their nests with fresh green leaves.

RED-SHOULDERED HAWK YEAR-ROUND

78

Kites

Male Snail Kite

SNAIL KITE

YEAR-ROUND

(FORMERLY CALLED EVERGLADES KITE)

Sighting the Snail Kite is a real treat for serious birders because it is so rare in the United States. As its name implies, it feeds on snails. It must have one particular species, the apple snail, a large snail found in the tall grasses of the wetlands. The Snail Kite is endangered in Florida because it is restricted to a small habitat which is itself threatened.

Not only does it require extensive fresh water marshes to supply Apple Snails, but, since it captures the snails with its talons, it needs low vegetation or numerous boat channels to be able to approach its prey from the air. The heavy airboat traffic around the Tamiami Trail helps beat down the tall grasses, and Snail Kites use these trails as foraging grounds.

Snail Kites are tropical birds from Central and South America that have established a slippery foothold in Florida.

Male

Female

Although once common in the Everglades, the Snail Kite population in Florida was estimated at a few dozen not long ago. Now there are probably 500 birds as the species makes a comeback. One likely place to see Snail Kites is around the restaurant run by the Miccosukee Indians along the Tamiami Trail.

79

Kites

SWALLOW-TAILED KITE   [SUMMER]

The Swallow-tailed Kite is easily recognized because it is the only Florida kite with a deeply forked tail. Its striking black and white color pattern also makes it stand out. Dozens of these birds can be seen around Clewiston in the summer.

The Swallow-tailed Kite stays airborne much of the time and drinks like a swallow by skimming over lakes and streams and scooping up water in its beak. One of its favorite foods is the very swift dragonfly. It also eats lizards, snakes, frogs, and nestling birds.

MISSISSIPPI KITE   [SUMMER]

▽ ▷ Central Florida is the southern end of the nesting range of this kite and it is rarely found in South Florida. The Mississippi Kite feeds on insects only, so small birds do not fear its presence. Notice the light-colored head and the dark tail that distinguishes this bird.

Just Like a Real Kite

The Swallow-tailed Kite can hover almost motionless in the air by setting its wings at the proper angle and flying directly into a good breeze.

Owls

In the United States, the owl is seen as a symbol of wisdom and knowledge. However, in the rest of the world the owl is regarded with fear as an omen of death and disaster. Most likely, this feeling comes from the fact that owls are birds of the night, and darkness is always scary. Their frightening shrieks and moans don't do much to dispel this negative image.

Owls have remarkable abilities which enable them to hunt in the dark. Their huge eyes allow them to see when other creatures cannot. The position of their eyes on the front of their heads gives them better binocular vision than many other birds whose eyes are on the sides of their heads. However, most owls hunt by sound. It is their keen, direction-finding sense of hearing that usually discovers the prey. That is why rodents, which rustle leaves as they walk around at night, are favorite targets.

GREAT HORNED OWL [YEAR-ROUND]

The Great Horned Owl is recognized by its large ear tufts and is sometimes called the "Cat Owl." Its large size enables it to consume a wide variety of prey. Skunks are a favorite food.

It occupies woodland areas, the same habitat as that of the Red-tailed Hawk. The two birds do not conflict with each other because the hawk hunts by day and the owl by night.

The Great Horned Owl is by far the largest and most powerful owl in Florida. It is even said to be able to hold its own in a confrontation with a Bald Eagle.

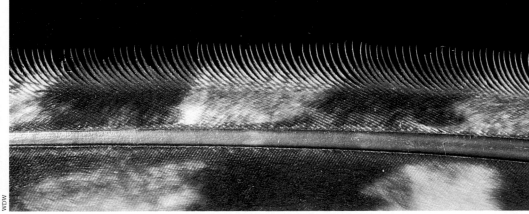

Owl feathers are specially adapted so that owls can fly silently and approach their prey without warning. The leading edge of an owl feather is unlike that of any other bird. The feather's edge is soft and downy, which eliminates the usual flapping noise of bird flight.

Owls

BARN OWL YEAR-ROUND

This owl cannot be mistaken because of its heart-shaped face and large disc shapes around the eyes. It is sometimes called the "monkey-faced" owl. The Barn Owl hunts mammals and is well respected by farmers for helping to control mice and rats.

The Barn Owl belongs to a different family than the other Florida owls. One difference is that the middle claw of the Barn Owl has a serrated, comb-like edge which is used for smoothing feathers.

The Barn Owl is found in almost every country of the world except the very cold northern countries. It is far more widespread than any other Florida owl. As its name implies, it likes to nest in man-made structures and is especially fond of barns and church steeples.

Young Barn Owls awaiting their parents

Crow harassing Barn Owl

Baby Barn Owl

The Barn Owl dines on small animals, especially rodents. It has to fear being eaten itself by the Great Horned Owl.

The Barn Owl does not "hoot" and it has been suggested that this owl should have been named "screech owl" because of its high-pitched cry.

BARRED OWL YEAR-ROUND

◁ This owl is recognized by the pattern of bars running across its chest and the contrasting streaks running down its belly. Barred Owls are quite abundant in Florida. Their habitat is the deep oak woods and cypress swamps.

Notice also the soft, dark-brown eyes. Barred Owls and Barn Owls are the only Florida owls with dark eyes.

COMMON SCREECH OWL `YEAR-ROUND`

The Common Screech Owl is Florida's smallest owl. The little screecher has "ear tufts," extra long bunches of feathers on both sides of the head. They are merely for show and do not aid the real ears, which are simply small openings hidden under the feathers. If you see a small owl and it has ear tufts, it must be a screech owl. The Great Horned Owl also has ear tufts, but is a much larger bird.

The screech owl usually does not screech but makes a soft, mournful sound. It is capable of a blood-curdling scream, but the scream is rarely heard. It captures all kinds of small prey and loves to eat palmetto bugs (those very large Florida roaches).

△ The screech owl has three color phases: brown, gray, and red. These variations may all occur in the same brood. According to one theory, if screech owls are living in various habitats, a variety of colors ensures that at least some of the birds will be well matched to their surroundings for camouflage. This may give the screech owls, as a group, an advantage for survival.

△ Common Screech Owl peering from its nest hole in a tree.

BURROWING OWL   YEAR-ROUND

Burrowing Owls are found on the open prairies of Central Florida and are sometimes found at airports and other grassy fields around the state. These owls excavate large burrows in the ground which serve as their homes. They are frequently seen standing in front of these burrows when not out foraging for prey, which includes insects and small animals.

While many owls are nocturnal, some, like the Burrowing Owl, are most active in the daytime. Birds that are active in the daytime are called "diurnal," and those active at night, "nocturnal."

◁ Digging its burrow, a determined owl makes the sand fly. This photo disproves a common myth that these birds only nest in gopher turtle holes and do not dig their own burrows.

△▷ Babies inside the burrow.

△ Angry Burrowing Owl tries to frighten an intruder with a threat display.

▷ Lazy days on the Kissimmee Prairie makes an owl sleepy.

△ Owls have the ability to rotate their heads a full 180 degrees so that they can look directly backwards. They can snap their heads around to the other side so quickly that the motion may not be noticed. That is why it appears that an owl can turn its head in endless circles.

△ Two heads are always better than one, and perhaps four eyes are better than two.

Vultures

Vultures are often mistakenly called buzzards. "Buzzard" is actually a European term for soaring hawks. Many of Florida's common hawks, such as the Red-shouldered Hawk, are members of this family of "buzzard hawks," also known as buteos. There are only two vulture species in the Eastern part of the United States, and both are common in Florida.

Unlike Bald Eagles which have white feathers on their heads, vultures really are bald. Their bare heads help keep them from getting too messy when they stick their necks deep into rotting carcasses.

Vultures are known as scavengers and eat dead animals almost exclusively although they will sometimes feed on garbage. It would be quite rare for a vulture to kill a healthy animal, but they do get impatient and will move in to dispatch an animal that is very sick or dying.

TURKEY VULTURE [YEAR-ROUND]

Birders sometimes call Turkey Vultures "TV's" for short. Turkey Vultures often dine on the squashed animals they find along highways, so, naturally, these delicacies are called "TV dinners."

Turkey Vultures are so-named because their red heads somewhat resemble the wattles of the Wild Turkey.

A Clothespin on the Nose?

Because of their grisly daily contact with dead animals, many people assume that vultures must have no sense of smell. However, experiments have shown that vultures have a very keen sense of smell. Vultures were able to locate dead animals from the air even though the carcasses were covered to prevent visual sighting.

The Skunks of the Bird World

Vultures have a unique defense mechanism. They vomit on would-be predators and their vomit is said to be so foul-smelling as to spoil the appetite of their assailants.

Vultures

Turkey Vultures roost together in groups, especially in the bare branches of dead trees. They leave their perches in the morning, but not as early as other birds. A few birds may remain at the roost during the day.

Young Turkey Vultures have black heads and can be mistaken for Black Vultures. Turkey Vultures are stronger fliers than Black Vultures. This allows the species to range up into more northerly states.

The Black Vulture is more confined to southern states where it can ride the thermal air currents which are abundant in warm climates.

Vultures

BLACK VULTURE

YEAR-ROUND

The Black Vulture is quite similar to the Turkey Vulture in its habits and the two birds often share the same roosts.

"There are many birds in this book I have never seen in my backyard!"

Many birds live in specific habitats such as open fields or deep woods. These birds do not vist backyards and the ambitious birder must seek them out. If you look in the right habitat at the right time of year, chances are good that you can see most of the birds in this book.